PRELUDE TO A KISS

AND OTHER PLAYS

CRAIG LUCAS

THEATRE COMMUNICATIONS GROUP
NEW YORK

This publication is made possible in part with public funds from the New York State Council on the Arts, a State Agency.

TCG books are exclusively distributed to the book trade by Consortium Book Sales and Distribution, 1045 Westgate Dr., St. Paul, MN 55114.

LIBRARY OF CONGRESS CATALOGING-IN-PUBLICATION DATA
Lucas, Craig
Prelude to a kiss and other plays / by Craig Lucas. — 1st ed.
p. cm.
Contents: Prelude to a kiss – Missing persons – Three postcards.
ISBN 1-55936-193-X (pbk. : alk. paper)
I. Title.
PS3562.U233 A6 2000
812'.54—dc21   00-04 6680

Cover design by Chip Kidd
Cover image is "Embrace," pencil, watercolor and gouache on paper, by Egon Schiele, 1912 and was provided by the Leopold Museum, Privatstiftung, Vienna
Text design and composition by Lisa Govan

First edition, October 2002

THIS VOLUME IS FOR MY MOTHERS:

ELEANORE, BEVERLY AND DOROTHY

■ CONTENTS ■

PRELUDE TO A KISS

This play is dedicated to my mother and father,
Charles and Eleanore Lucas

Prelude to a Kiss was commissioned by South Coast Repertory (David Emmes, Producing Artistic Director; Martin Benson, Artistic Director) in Costa Mesa, California, where it premiered on January 15, 1988. It was directed by Norman René; the set design was by Loy Arcenas, the costume design was by Walker Hicklin, the lighting design was by Peter Maradudin, the sound design was by Serge Ossorguine, the dramaturg was John Glore and the stage manager was Julie Haber. The cast was as follows:

PETER	Mark Arnott
TAYLOR	Michael Canavan
RITA	Lisa Zane
TOM	Art Koustik
MRS. BOYLE	Teri Ralston
DR. BOYLE	Hal Landon, Jr.
MINISTER	John-David Keller
AUNT DOROTHY	Roberta Farkas
OLD MAN	Frank Hamilton
LEAH	Mary Anne McGarry
ENSEMBLE	Lisa Black, Cynthia Blaise, Edgar W. Chambers, Patrick Massoth, Roberta Ornellas, Paul J. Read, Catherine Rowe
*GINNY	Roberta Farkas
*NANCY	Anni Long
*FAMILY FRIEND	Anni Long
*FAMILY FRIEND'S HUSBAND	Don Took

(*Roles cut from present version)

A revised version of *Prelude to a Kiss* premiered at Circle Repertory Company (Tanya Berezin, Artistic Director; Connie L. Alexis, Managing Director) in New York City on March 14, 1990. It was directed by Norman René; the set design was by Loy Arcenas, the costume design was by Walker Hicklin, the lighting design was by Debra J. Kletter, the sound design was by Scott Lehrer, the hair and wig design was by Bobby H. Grayson and the stage manager was M. A. Howard. The cast was as follows:

PETER	Alec Baldwin
TAYLOR	John Dossett
RITA	Mary-Louise Parker
TOM	L. Peter Callender
MRS. BOYLE	Debra Monk
DR. BOYLE	Larry Bryggman
MINISTER	Craig Bockhorn
AUNT DOROTHY	Joyce Reehling
UNCLE FRED	Michael Warren Powell
OLD MAN	Barnard Hughes
JAMAICAN WAITER	L. Peter Callender
LEAH	Joyce Reehling
ENSEMBLE	Kimberly Dudwitt, Pete Tyler

Prelude to a Kiss opened on Broadway at the Helen Hayes
Theater on May 1, 1990. It was produced by Christopher
Gould, Suzanne Golden and Dodger Productions. It was
directed by Norman René; the set design was by Loy Arcenas,
the costume design was by Walker Hicklin, the lighting
design was by Debra J. Kletter, the sound design was by
Scott Lehrer, the hair and wig design was by Bobby H.
Grayson and the stage manager was James Harker. The cast
was as follows:

PETER	Timothy Hutton
TAYLOR	John Dossett
RITA	Mary-Louise Parker
TOM	L. Peter Callender
MRS. BOYLE	Debra Monk
DR. BOYLE	Larry Bryggman
MINISTER	Craig Bockhorn
AUNT DOROTHY	Joyce Reehling
UNCLE FRED	Michael Warren Powell
OLD MAN	Barnard Hughes
JAMAICAN WAITER	L. Peter Callender
LEAH	Joyce Reehling
ENSEMBLE	Craig Bockhorn, Brian Cousins, Kimberly Dudwitt, Michael Warren Powell

■ CHARACTERS ■

PETER

TAYLOR

RITA

TOM

MRS. BOYLE

DR. BOYLE

MINISTER

AUNT DOROTHY

UNCLE FRED

OLD MAN

JAMAICAN WAITER

LEAH

PARTY GUESTS, BARFLIES,
WEDDING GUESTS, VACATIONERS

Then the king's daughter began to weep
and was afraid of the cold frog,
whom nothing would satisfy
but he must sleep
in her pretty clean bed.

—BROTHERS GRIMM,
The Frog Prince

Death destroys a man,
but the idea of death is
what saves him.

—E. M. FORSTER,
Howard's End

■ ACT ONE ■

We hear a recorded vocalist as the lights go down: "If you hear a song in blue, / Like a flower crying for the dew, / That was my heart serenading you, / My prelude to a kiss."
A crowded party. Peter stands apart, then approaches Taylor.

PETER: I'm splitting . . . Hey, Tay?

TAYLOR: Hey, Pete, did you meet Rita?

PETER: No. Hi.

RITA: Hi.

TAYLOR *(Overlapping)*: Rita, Peter, Peter, Rita.

PETER: Actually, I . . .

TAYLOR *(Overlapping)*: What's everybody drinking? Reet? Can I fill you up there?

RITA: Oh, I'll have another Dewar's, thanks.

TAYLOR: Pete?

PETER: No, nothing, thank—

TAYLOR: Don't worry, I've got it taken care of. You two just relax. One Dewar's, one beer . . .

(Taylor moves off. Pause.)

PETER: How do you know the Sokols?

RITA: I don't. I mean, except from the hall.

PETER: Oh, you're a neighbor.

RITA: I couldn't sleep.

PETER: Oh, really? Why? . . . How long have you lived here?

RITA: I haven't slept since I was fourteen. A year and a half.

(Beat.)

PETER: Did you say you hadn't slept since you were fourteen?

RITA: Pretty much.

PETER: You look great!

RITA: Thank you.

PETER: Considering. Rita what?

RITA: Boyle.

PETER: Peter Hoskins.

RITA: Hoskins?

PETER: As in Hoskin's disease?

RITA: Oh, Hodgkin's.

PETER: No, no, it was just a . . . nonhumorous . . . flail.

RITA: What?

(Peter shakes his head.)

I like your shirt!

(Taylor returns with drinks.)

TAYLOR: Dewar's, madame?

RITA: Thank you.

TAYLOR: No beer, sorry.

PETER: Wine's fine. Thanks . . . Rita has insomnia.

TAYLOR: Oh yeah? Listen, I've got to pee, I'm sorry, excuse
me. Forgive me . . . *(He is gone again)*

PETER: What do you do when you're not NOT sleeping?

RITA: Oh, I usually, you know . . . write in my journal or—
. . . Oh, for a living, you mean? I'm a bartender.

PETER: Oh. Where?

RITA *(Overlapping)*: Yeah. At the Tin Market.

PETER: Oh, I know where that is. One for Pete.

RITA: Yeah.

PETER: I guess it's a good place for an insomniac to work. You work Saturdays?

(She nods.)

Well, you must make good money. Well, so you hate it, I'm sorry, I can't help that. What are your aspirations, in that case?

RITA: I'm like a graphic designer.

PETER: Oh, great.

RITA: I studied at Parsons.

PETER: This is good.

RITA: What do you do?

PETER: I make little, tiny, transparent photographs of scientific articles which are rolled on film like microfilm only smaller. You'd like it. It's really interesting.

RITA: What are your aspirations in that case?

PETER: I should have some, shouldn't I? No, I, I, I, I, I, I, uh, can't think of the answer, I'm sorry.

RITA: That's okay!

PETER: So why can't you sleep? You know what's good? I forget what it's called, it's an herb.

RITA: I tried it.

PETER: It didn't work?

RITA: I can't remember what it's called either. My memory is terrible!

PETER: Maybe that's why you can't sleep. You forget how tired you are. Well . . . If you ever need any help getting to sleep. *(Beat)* Sorry. *(Beat)* It was nice talking to you.

RITA: You, too.

PETER: Get some sleep.

RITA: I'll try.

(Peter addresses the audience:)

PETER: I stood outside for a while, just listening to the silence. Then I tried to figure out which window was hers and what her life might be like and why she couldn't sleep. Like that. *(Beat)* The spell was cast.

(The scene changes to the Tin Market.)

PETER: Hi.
RITA: Oh, hi.
PETER: Is this all right?
RITA: No, I'm sorry, you can never come in here . . . What's new?
PETER: Since yesterday? Well, let's see, so much has happened. You look great.
RITA: What'll you drink?
PETER: Do you have Molson? . . .

(She nods.)

So, did you get some sleep?
RITA: Eventually. *(She sets down his Molson)*
PETER: Thank you.
RITA: You?
PETER: Sleep? Oh, I don't have any trouble. But . . . let's see, I read *The White Hotel* today.
RITA: Oh.
PETER: That was pretty much it.
RITA: Yeah.
PETER: You?
RITA: Oh, I slept, mostly . . . How was *The White Hotel?*
PETER: Did you read it?
RITA: No, but I've read some of the case histories it's based on.
PETER: You have? Freud's? Case histories? You've read Freud.
RITA: Have you?
PETER: No, but . . . This book?
RITA: Uh-huh?

PETER: Starts with this very highfalutin sexual dream thing, you know?

RITA: Yeah, I've heard everybody beats off when they read it.

(Beat.)

PETER: Uh-huh.

RITA: I'm sorry.

PETER: You heard that?

RITA: Go on.

PETER: . . . It's very depressing, the book.

RITA: Uh-huh.

PETER: This lovely, very neurotic woman goes into therapy with Freud himself—

RITA: Right.

PETER: And he sort of cures her so that she can go on to live for a few years before being killed by the Nazis in a lime pit. Happy. Happy stuff.

RITA: So why were you in Europe for ten years?

PETER: How did you know I was in Europe?

RITA: Word gets around.

PETER: You asked Taylor about me? You were asking around about me? Let's get married.

RITA: Okay.

PETER: I just went, you know.

RITA: He said there was a story and you would have to tell me.

PETER: He did? . . . Okay, this is the story and I'm not making this up.

RITA: Okay.

PETER: And it's not as sad as it sounds.

RITA: Shoot.

PETER: My parents?

RITA: Uh-huh?

PETER: Separated when I was four. And I went to live with my grandparents who are unfortunately deceased now. I'm going to make this as brief as possible.

RITA: Take your time.

PETER: And—

RITA: We can go up to my place if you want. When you're done.

PETER: And-everything-worked-out-great-for-everybody-it-was-amazing.

RITA: No, go on.

PETER: Were you serious about that?

RITA: I'm off in about seven minutes. Your parents.

PETER: My parents. I'm four years old. I go to live with my grandparents. My grandfather had to go into a nursing home when I was nine, then my grandmother had to go when I was eleven; they were both sick, so I go to live with my mother, who by this time is remarried to Hank.

RITA: Uh-huh.

PETER: Very unhappy person, ridicules me in front of the other two children they have created from their unsavory loins, so I go to live with my father, who is also remarried, three other children; Sophie, the new wife, hates me even more than Hank.

RITA: This is like Dickens.

PETER: The only nice thing Sophie ever did for me was make the same food twice when I had made the mistake of saying I liked it. Usually she would stop cooking whatever it was I said I liked.

RITA: What was it?

PETER: What I liked? Spaetzles?

RITA: Oh god.

PETER: You've had spaetzles?

RITA: Oh, sure.

PETER: You like them?

RITA: I love them.

PETER: You do?

RITA: Uh-huh. Anyway.

PETER: You love spaetzles. Anyway, everyone is unhappy now.

RITA: Uh-huh.

PETER: Sophie really can't stand the sight of me, because I remind her that my father was married to someone else and . . .

RITA: Right.

PETER: And my father does not seem too fond of me, either. I don't know if he ever was, but, so one night I say I'm going to go to the movies and instead I go to Europe.

RITA: What movie?

PETER: *The Wild Bunch*, I think, why?

RITA: Did you call them first?

PETER: Not until I got there.

RITA: Europe?

PETER: And I called collect.

RITA: That is . . .

PETER: Yeah.

RITA: Good for you.

PETER: Yeah. So. Why'd you ask which movie?

RITA: That is fabulous.

PETER: That's the story.

RITA: How did you eat? I mean . . .

PETER: Oh, I had about three thousand dollars saved up from my paper route. But that's a whole other kettle of . . .

RITA: Spaetzles.

PETER: Yeah. So . . .

RITA: You lived in Amsterdam?

PETER: You're a spy, aren't you?

(Tom, another bartender, enters behind the bar.)

TOM: Hey, kiddo.

RITA: Hi. Tom, this is Peter.

TOM: Hi.

PETER: Good to meet you.

RITA *(To Peter)*: You want to go?

PETER: Now? Naaaaaaaa. *(To us)* I love the little sign when you buy your ticket to the roller coaster: RIDE AT YOUR OWN RISK. As if the management is not at all concerned with your safety, the entire contraption is about to collapse and, to top it off, there are supernatural powers out there just waiting to pull you off the tracks and out into, you know, your worst, cruelest nightmare—the wild blue. They want you to believe that anything can happen. *(Beat)* And they're right.

(Peter and Rita are outside. They walk.)

PETER: Uh-huh.

RITA: So.

PETER: So they disowned you?

RITA: No. I never told them.

PETER: Oh.

RITA: It was like . . . I mean, they didn't need to know what I was involved with. I don't tell them everything.

PETER: I've never known a Communist.

RITA: Socialist.

PETER: Socialist.

RITA: But . . . I mean, I was only in the Party for about two months.

PETER: What happened?

RITA: Oh, I just . . . I felt like they were basically not interested in anything except being right.

PETER: Right.

RITA: And they didn't support the Soviet Union, not that they should—

PETER: Uh-huh.

RITA: —and they didn't support Mao, and they didn't support the United States. It's like where are you going to live?

PETER: Right.

RITA: But . . . I started by doing leaflets for them and then posters. I still did that after I left. What?

PETER: Nothing.

RITA: It was such a strange time . . . You're a good listener.

PETER: So now you're . . .

RITA: Oh, I guess I'm a Democrat.

PETER: Me, too.

RITA: But . . . they're such Republicans.

PETER: Your parents?

RITA: No, the Democrats. Beneath the skin.

PETER: Oh, uh-huh?

RITA: But . . . I don't know. I guess it's like the U.S. It isn't perfect.

PETER: Right. *(Pause)* Where do they live?

RITA: My parents? Englewood Cliffs. It's right across the bridge. It's nice, actually.

PETER: What do they do?

RITA: My dad's a dentist.

PETER: Oh, really?

RITA: Uh-huh.

PETER: Wow.

RITA: Why?

PETER: No, I just think that's . . . interesting.

RITA: It is?

PETER: I think so. I don't know.

RITA: My mother's a mother.

PETER: Do you have brothers and sisters?

(She shakes her head.)

They must dote on you.

RITA: What's Amsterdam like? D'you speak Dutch?

PETER: Ja.

RITA: Say something in Dutch.

PETER: Uh . . . *Je hebt erg witte tanden.*

RITA: What's that?

PETER: You have very white teeth.

RITA: Oh. Thank you.

PETER: Now you say, *Om je better mee op te eten.*

RITA: What is it?

PETER: *Om je better mee op te eten.*

RITA: *Om je metter—*

PETER: *Better . . .*

RITA: *Better . . .*

PETER: . . . *mee op te eten.*

RITA: . . . *mee op te eten.*

PETER: *Om je better mee op te eten.*

RITA: *Om je better mee op te eten.*

PETER: Great. You've got a good ear.

RITA: Oh. Good ear, clean teeth.

PETER: You do.

RITA: What did I say?

PETER: I can't tell you.

RITA *(Overlapping)*: I knew you were gonna say that, I knew it!

PETER: No, it's untranslatable.

RITA: I'm sure it is. No, come on.

PETER: I'll tell you someday. . . .

RITA: So what did you do there?

PETER: In Amsterdam? I will, I promise.

RITA: How old were you when you went?

PETER: Sixteen.

RITA: Oh, wow.

PETER: I catered for the first couple of years and made sandwiches during the day; then I tutored rich little cutiepies on their English and went to school at night. Finally I came back when my dad died.

(Pause.)

RITA: Do you see your mom or your family at all?

(He shakes his head.)

Never?

PETER: Nope.

RITA: Do you call them?

(He shakes his head.)

You miss them?

(He shakes his head. Pause.
Scene changes to Rita's apartment.)

PETER: This is great.

RITA: You want a Molson?

PETER: You drink Molson—

RITA: Uh-huh.

PETER: —in your own home?

RITA: I've been known to.

PETER: That's really . . .

RITA: A coincidence.

PETER: A coincidence. So why can't you sleep? I want to solve this.

RITA: I really wasn't exaggerating. It's been since I was fourteen.

PETER: That's a lot of journal-keeping . . . Have you seen doctors?

RITA: I've seen all the doctors.

PETER: Uh-huh.

RITA: Of every known . . .

PETER: Right.

RITA *(Overlapping)*: Persuasion. I've ingested countless . . .
  (She hands him a Molson)

PETER: Thanks.

RITA: Pills, liquids, I've seen an acupuncturist.

PETER: You did? What did it feel like?

RITA: Little needles in your back.

PETER: It hurt?

RITA: Sometimes.

PETER: They always lie.

RITA: I know.

PETER: You're really beautiful.

(She laughs.)

You are.

RITA: Thank you. That's . . . No, thank you.

(They kiss. She laughs.)

PETER: This is not supposed to be the funny part.

RITA: No, I know, I'm sorry . . . I'm, I guess I'm nervous.

PETER: Why are you nervous? Don't be nervous.

RITA: All right.

(He approaches to kiss her.)

PETER: Don't laugh . . . All right, you can laugh.

(They kiss.)

Am I going too fast?

(She shakes her head.)

Is this tacky of me?

(Head shake.)

Oh good.

(They kiss.)

This is definitely the highlight of my weekend.

(She smiles.)

So maybe we should just, you know, watch some TV, have happy memories of this and anticipate the future—

(She is shaking her head.)

—we shouldn't?

(They kiss.)

I would really, really like to see you with all of your clothes off and stuff like that.

RITA: I would really, really like to see you with all of your clothes off and . . .

PETER: Stuff like that? *(To us)* When you're first getting to know someone and in that blissful, psychotic first flush of love, it seems like every aspect of their personality, their whole demeanor, the simple, lovely twist of their earlobes and their marvelous phone voice and their soft, dark wet whatever is somehow imbued with an extra push of color, an intensity heretofore . . . you know. Unknown.

(Rita's apartment. Later.)

PETER: Christ!

RITA: What?

PETER: Happiness! . . . Are you?

RITA: Uh-huh.

PETER: You are? It's like a drug.

RITA: It is a drug.

PETER: Sex?

RITA: To snare us into mating.

PETER: I must be peaking then.

RITA: No, the body manufactures it.

PETER: Uh-huh.

RITA: Like epinephrine or something.

PETER: Maybe that's where they got the word "crack."

RITA: Shut up. I prefer hole. Frankly.

PETER: Hole?

RITA: And dick.

PETER: Slit.

RITA: Ugh.

PETER: This is sick.

RITA: Tool, I like.

PETER: Uh-huh.

RITA: It's practical.

PETER: Wait a minute, did I detect an earlier note of cynicism in your comment about mating?

RITA: Oh. No.

PETER: You don't like kids?

RITA: No, I love them.

PETER: But you don't want to have them?

RITA: No, I don't, but . . .

PETER: Why not?

RITA: I just don't.

PETER: Your career?

RITA: What career? No, I think kids are great, I just don't think it's fair to raise them in the world. The way it is now.

PETER: Where else are you going to raise them? We're here.

RITA: I know, but . . .

PETER: It's like what you were saying about the Socialists.

(Rita hesitates.)

Say.

RITA: Like . . . the woman in *The White Hotel*. People really do struggle their whole lives just to die in lime pits, and not just in books. Women go blind from watching their children being murdered.

PETER: Not in this country they don't.

RITA: No, they get shot on the sidewalk in front of their houses in some drug war. I mean, just what you went through being passed from one parent to another who didn't even—

PETER: I survived . . .

(Pause.)

RITA: I'll be lying in bed late at night and I'll look at the light in the room and suddenly see it all just go up in a blinding flash, in flames, and I'm the only one left alive . . . I can't look at you sitting there without imagining you . . . dying . . . bursting into flames . . .

PETER: No wonder you can't sleep.

RITA: The world's a really terrible place. It's too precarious. *(Pause)* You want kids, obviously. I wish I could say I did.

PETER: It's okay.

RITA: What's your dirtiest fantasy?

PETER: Excuse me? No, I thought you just said what's my dirtiest fantasy.

RITA: What?

PETER: No, I can't—

RITA: Yes, you can. Please?

PETER: I'm sorry, I can't. What's yours, though? I'd be curious.

RITA *(Overlapping)*: I asked you first. Come on.

PETER: Oh god.

RITA: Please.

PETER: Well, they change.

RITA: Sure. What's one?

PETER: One?

RITA: Uh-huh.

PETER: Well . . . One?

RITA: Uh-huh.

PETER: Might be that someone . . . you know—

RITA: Uh-huh.

PETER: —who might just happen to be around the apartment—

RITA: Uh-huh.

PETER *(Mimicking her)*: Uh-huh, uh-huh. Might . . . sort of just, you know, spontaneously start crawling across the floor—

RITA: Uh-huh.

PETER: —on their hands and knees and . . . more or less unzip me with their, uh . . . teeth.

RITA: I'd do that.

PETER: You would?

RITA: Uh-huh.

PETER: Right now? *(She nods)*

(To us) We saw each other every night for the next six weeks. And it wasn't just the knees and the teeth, despite what you think. I would stop by my apartment now and then to see if the view out onto the airshaft had improved any, but my clothes had all found their way over to Rita's and my books.

And then . . .

(Rita's apartment. Six weeks later. Peter is serving dinner.)

PETER: That was the Communist?

RITA: Socialist.

PETER: Socialist.

RITA: No. That was the one who liked to dress up, go out.

PETER: Oh, right. But you don't like to go dancing, do you?

RITA: Sometimes. I change.

PETER: Uh-huh.

RITA: People do.

PETER: So before that was the Communist?

RITA: Socialist.

PETER *(Overlapping)*: Socialist. And before that? . . .

RITA: Oh, it was just high school, you know. This looks great.
No, wait, there was someone else, who was it?

PETER: Is that what's going to happen to me?

RITA: Oh no—John—I told you about John.

PETER: The one who wanted to run away with you? Is that
what's going to happen to me?

RITA: You're gonna want to run away?

PETER: You're going to forget my name over dinner with someone else equally enamored of you and just attribute it
to your lousy memory? "Oh, yes, that's right—Peter.
Peter—"

RITA: Probably.

PETER: "What did he look like?" And then you'll tell them
my dirtiest fantasy and how you degraded yourself just
for a home-cooked meal.

RITA: Mmmm.

(They start to eat.)

I told my parents about you.

PETER: What did you tell them?

RITA: I said that you were very considerate.

PETERr: In what way?

RITA: I said—well, I mean, we talk very frankly about sex.

PETER: You and your parents?

RITA: And I said that you always brought protection . . .

PETER: You did not.

RITA: And that you were very attentive to whether or not I had an orgasm.

PETER: This is such bullshit.

RITA: No, I said they should meet you, what do you think?

PETER: Protection.

RITA: They're nice.

PETER: I'm sure.

RITA: So are you free this weekend?

PETER: Sure.

RITA: Don't be nervous.

PETER: All right. Did you tell them about my family and everything?

RITA: My mother.

PETER: She knows the story?

RITA: Uh-huh.

PETER: All about me?

RITA: Uh-huh.

PETER: Will you marry me?

RITA: Uh-huh.

PETER: You will?

RITA: Uh-huh.

(Beat.)

PETER: I just wanted to see how it sounds.

RITA: It sounds great.

PETER: This is too fast. Isn't it?

RITA: Is it?

PETER: I don't think so.

RITA: Neither do I.

PETER: You'll marry me?

RITA: Uh-huh.

PETER: You will?

RITA: Uh-huh.

(The Boyle home. Doorbell.)

RITA: Mom?

MRS. BOYLE: Nice to meet you.

RITA: Dad.

PETER: Dr. Boyle.

RITA: These are my parents . . .

MRS. BOYLE: So I understand you're a manager in a publishing firm.

PETER: That's correct. Yes.

DR. BOYLE: That must be, uh . . . What kind of firm is it?

MRS. BOYLE: Publishing.

DR. BOYLE: What kind—don't belittle me in front of new people.

MRS. BOYLE: Belittle?

RITA: Dad, please.

DR. BOYLE: What kind of publishing firm is it? I was asking.

PETER: It's, uh, scientific publishing. They publish, you know, scientific publishing—things—journals! I knew I knew that.

RITA *(To Peter)*: You want a beer?

PETER: Sure.

MRS. BOYLE: In the morning, Rita?

RITA: Yes, Mother, we have been drinking nonstop for weeks, it's time you knew this about us.

MRS. BOYLE: I'll have one too, then.

RITA: You will?

DR. BOYLE: Me, too.

PETER: A bunch of lushes here, Rita, you didn't tell me.

DR. BOYLE: Oh, I can pull out four wisdom teeth on a fifth of Stoli.

PETER: You can?

MRS. BOYLE: He's teasing you.

DR. BOYLE: Scien—what kind of scientific?

PETER: Abstracting and indexing. It's a service.

DR. BOYLE: Like a database.

PETER: It is a database.

DR. BOYLE: It is a database. Covering . . . ?

PETER: All kinds of fields.

DR. BOYLE: All kinds.

PETER: Pretty much, you know, everything from energy to robotics to medical articles. I've memorized our marketing material.

DR. BOYLE: I've seen this.

(Rita hands everyone his/her beer.)

PETER: Thank you.

(They clink bottles.)

DR. BOYLE: I've seen this sort of thing.

PETER: Yeah.

DR. BOYLE: So you're the manager . . . ?

PETER: The manager of the fiche department.

DR. BOYLE: Microfiche.

PETER: Right.

MRS. BOYLE: The, what is it?

DR. BOYLE: Microfiche.

PETER: It's like microfilm only smaller.

MRS. BOYLE: Uh-huh.

PETER: Little film.

DR. BOYLE: Why do you do that?

PETER: Microfiche?

DR. BOYLE: No, why does the company do microfiche?

PETER: Oh, I see. Because if you want to call up and—

DR. BOYLE: Oh, I—yes, yes, yes, yes, yes.

PETER *(Overlapping)*: —ask for like—

DR. BOYLE: Right, a certain article.

PETER: Right. We can retrieve it for you. And we also film the abstract journals we actually publish so . . .

DR. BOYLE: To save space.

PETER: Right. Yes, in libraries, it saves space.

DR. BOYLE: All right. We approve.

RITA: Daddy.

MRS. BOYLE: Marshall.

DR. BOYLE: Maybe now she'll get some sleep.

MRS. BOYLE: Now how long have you two been going out?

RITA: Over a year now.

(Peter looks at Rita; a beat.)

PETER: About that. Yeah.
MRS. BOYLE: Rita says you've been abroad.
PETER: Yes, I have.
MRS. BOYLE: Where?
PETER: Amsterdam, for the most part, but...
MRS. BOYLE: Marshall was in Korea.
PETER: Oh, was it nice? Oh, no, no, I see—
MRS. BOYLE: Nice!
DR. BOYLE: Some people might have been able to relax, I don't know, bullets flying.
PETER *(Overlapping)*: Right. Right.
MRS. BOYLE: We're playing with you.
DR. BOYLE: Okay, here you go.

(Dr. Boyle starts to untuck his shirttail.)

RITA: Oh no, Daddy, please, god, please—
DR. BOYLE *(Overlapping)*: This is the only scar you'll ever see in the shape of a saxophone.
MRS. BOYLE: It really is, people think he's kidding.
PETER: Really?
DR. BOYLE: If he's going to be in the family, he's got to see these things.

(The Boyle home. A month later.)

PETER *(To us, as he changes into his wedding garb)*: I stood in front of the full-length mirror in their upstairs guest room, looking out over the yard at the little tent and the band and the food which had been catered; I felt a certain kinship with these people, the caterers.

(Rita sneaks up, covers his eyes.)

RITA: Don't look, it's bad luck.

PETER: All right, but—wait, wait—you don't believe that, do you?

RITA *(Overlapping)*: You looked.

PETER: I didn't look.

RITA: You're looking.

PETER: Wait, I won't look. I won't.

RITA *(Overlapping)*: No, you've already cursed the first fourteen years of our marriage.

PETER: I love you.

RITA: What about when I'm a hundred years old with a moustache and yellow teeth?

PETER: I'll still love you.

RITA: And I'm sagging down to here and I'm bald?

PETER: I'll love you all the more.

RITA: Are you sure?

PETER: Yes, I promise.

RITA: And I won't ever want to make love and I can never remember anything?

PETER: You can never remember anything now.

RITA: That's true. Okay.

(She leaves; Peter's eyes remain closed.)

PETER: What about me?

(Taylor comes in with two beers; he is wearing sunglasses.)

TAYLOR: What about you? . . . You okay?

PETER: Great, Taylor.

TAYLOR: They're holding for the musicians.

PETER: Okay.

(Taylor helps Peter dress.)

TAYLOR: Now listen. There's nothing at all to worry about here.

PETER: I know that.

TAYLOR: This is a natural step in life's plan. Like sliding down a banister.

PETER: Right.

TAYLOR: That turns into a razor blade. No, I don't want you to think of this as anything more than one of the little skirmishes we all wage, each and every day of our lives, in the eternal struggle against mediocrity and decay. Straighten your tie.

PETER: I straightened my tie.

TAYLOR: Fix your face. You're not compromising yourself.

PETER: Thank you.

TAYLOR: Not at all. You see all those middle-aged guys down there in their checked pants and their wives in the flouncy dresses?

PETER: Mm-hm.

TAYLOR: They were all very hip once. But . . . There's the music. You okay?

PETER: Just go.

TAYLOR: Relax. I've got the ring.

PETER: Great. Go.

(Taylor kisses Peter on the cheek; mouths, "I love you."
The Boyle home. Outside.)

MINISTER: . . . to keep the solemn vows you are about to make. Live with tender consideration for each other. Conduct your lives in honesty and in truth. And your marriage will last. This should be remembered as you now declare your desire to be wed.

PETER: I, Peter, take thee, Rita, to be my wedded wife, to have and to hold from this day forward, for better or for worse, for richer or for poorer, in sickness and in health, to love and to cherish, till death us do part, according to God's holy ordinance; and thereto, I pledge thee my troth.

RITA: I, Rita, take thee, Peter, to be my wedded husband, to have and to hold from this day forward, for better or for worse, for richer or for poorer, *(Halting)* in sick-

ness and in health, to love and to cherish, till death us
do part, according to God's holy ordinance; and thereto, I pledge thee my troth.

MINISTER: For as much as Rita and Peter have consented
together in holy matrimony and have witnessed the
same before God and this company, pledging their
faith and declaring the same, I pronounce, by the
authority committed unto me as a minister of God,
that they are husband and wife, according to the ordinance of God and the law of this state, in the name of
the Father, and of the Son, and of the Holy Spirit . . .

(Peter and Rita kiss.)

I think a little applause would be in order.

PETER *(To us)*: And there was some polite applause as if we'd
made a good putt or something, and we all made a
beeline for the champagne with the strawberries in it.

(The Boyle home; outside. Later that day.)

RITA: Peter, you remember my Aunt Dorothy and Uncle
Fred.

PETER: Yes, good to see you.

UNCLE FRED: Peter and Rita, that's very euphonious.

PETER: Yes.

AUNT DOROTHY: Isn't it?

RITA: Sometimes we get Peter and Reeter.

AUNT DOROTHY: Oh.

RITA: Or Pita and Rita.

PETER: Excuse me, Rita, who's the guy in the green coat?
Over by the food?

RITA: Oh . . . *(She sees the Old Man)* Oh, yeah. I don't know.

MRS. BOYLE: Everybody shmush together, come on! Marshall! . . .

(People crowd together around Peter and Rita.)

Marshall!

DR. BOYLE: What?

MRS. BOYLE: Get in the picture, come on!

DR. BOYLE: Jesus Christ, I thought you were on fire.

MRS. BOYLE: Get in, everybody! All right. Say: "Bullshit!" Smile!

(Everyone says, "Bullshit" and/or "Cheese." Flash.)

DR. BOYLE: Don't tell her—

MRS. BOYLE: Wait, I want to get another one. Don't move. Ohhhhh.

DR. BOYLE *(Overlapping, continuous from earlier line)*: —you don't need a flashbulb in the middle of the day.

UNCLE FRED: My face hurts, hurry up!

MRS. BOYLE: All right, say, "Bullshit."

(Again.)

AUNT DOROTHY: Oh, I had my face in a funny position.

UNCLE FRED: Whose fault is that?

AUNT DOROTHY: And don't say it's always that way.

PETER: Mom, who's the guy over by the bar?

MRS. BOYLE: Who?

PETER: See who I mean?

MRS. BOYLE: Oh . . .

(Rita and the Old Man toast one another with their champagne.)

RITA: Isn't he great?

MRS. BOYLE: No, I thought he was with your firm.

PETER *(Shaking his head)*: Unh-uh.

(The Old Man starts toward them.)

MRS. BOYLE: Marsh? Right behind me, don't look now, he's very peculiar.

DR. BOYLE: Never seen him before in my life.

MRS. BOYLE: He's not with the club, is he?

(The Old Man comes up to them.)

OLD MAN: Congratulations. Both of you.
RITA: Thank you.
PETER: Thank you very much.
TAYLOR *(Extending his hand)*: I'm Taylor McGowan.
OLD MAN: You make a lovely couple.
TAYLOR: Your name, I'm sorry?
OLD MAN: And what a wonderful day for it.
RITA *(Mesmerized by him)*: Yes.

(Taylor shakes hands with the empty air.)

TAYLOR: Good to meet you.
OLD MAN: How precious the time is . . . How little we realize
   till it's almost gone.
DR. BOYLE: You'll have to forgive us, but none of us seems to
   remember who you are.
RITA: It's all right, Daddy.
OLD MAN: I only wanted to wish the two young people well.
   And perhaps to kiss the bride. Before I'm on my way.
DR. BOYLE: Well—
RITA: I'd be flattered. Thank you.
TAYLOR: Some angle this guy's got.
RITA: My blessings to you.

*(The Old Man takes Rita's face in his hands. There is a
low rumble which grows in volume as they begin to kiss.
Wind rushes through the trees, leaves fall, no one moves
except for Rita, whose bridal bouquet slips to the ground.
The Old Man and Rita separate, and the wind and rumble die down.)*

RITA: And you.

(The Old Man seems off balance; Dr. Boyle steadies him.)

DR. BOYLE: Do you want to sit down?
AUNT DOROTHY: Get him a chair, Fred.
TAYLOR: Too much blood rushing to the wrong place, I guess.

(The Old Man stares at Peter and Rita.)

DR. BOYLE: Are you dizzy?
OLD MAN: Peter? . . .

(Uncle Fred brings a chair.)

DR. BOYLE: Here you go now.

(He eases the Old Man into the chair, takes his pulse. Peter remains fixated on the Old Man. Rita has withdrawn from the crowd; she examines her dress, her hands, the air around her, as if it were all new, miraculous.)

MRS. BOYLE: I thought you said you didn't know him.

(Peter is mystified.)

Peter?
DR. BOYLE: Take it easy now.

OLD MAN *(To Peter)*: Honey?
Honey? . . . It's me.
What's happening? . . .
Why is . . . ? Why is   DR. BOYLE: You're okay now,
everybody . . . ?   just breathe for me,
                                   nice and easy.

OLD MAN *(Staring at Dr. Boyle)*: Daddy, it's me.
AUNT DOROTHY: Ohhhh, he thinks Marshall's his father.
TAYLOR: Where do you live, can you tell us?
DR. BOYLE: Okay. He's doing fine. Everybody relax.
AUNT DOROTHY: Get him a glass of water, Fred.

DR. BOYLE: He's had too much to drink, I suspect. Am I right? A little too much champagne?

(The Old Man begins to nod, strangely.)

MRS. BOYLE: Should I call an ambulance? Marshall?
DR. BOYLE: No, no. He's going to be fine.
OLD MAN: I've had too much to drink.
DR. BOYLE: That's right. Somebody get him a cup of coffee.

(Uncle Fred arrives with water.)

AUNT DOROTHY: Coffee, make it coffee.

(Uncle Fred exits.)

MRS. BOYLE: Where do you live, can you tell us?
OLD MAN: Please . . .
MRS. BOYLE: Is there someone we can call?
OLD MAN: I'm sorry for any trouble I've caused.

(The Old Man starts to stand.)

DR. BOYLE: There's no trouble.
MRS. BOYLE: Don't let him, honey—
DR. BOYLE *(Overlapping)*: We just want to see you don't hurt yourself.
UNCLE FRED *(Returning with coffee)*: Here you go.
OLD MAN *(Backing away)*: No, thank you.
UNCLE FRED: Don't burn yourself.
OLD MAN: No.
AUNT DOROTHY: He doesn't want it, Fred.
MRS. BOYLE: Don't just let him wander off is all I'm saying.
DR. BOYLE: All right, Marion—
MRS. BOYLE: He could fall and he could hurt himself, that's all—
DR. BOYLE: He's not going to sue us, trust me.

(Dr. Boyle and Taylor follow the Old Man off.)

MRS. BOYLE: And find out where he lives!

UNCLE FRED: He'll be fine.

AUNT DOROTHY: I'm sure he's a neighbor or someone's gardener.

MRS. BOYLE: Whose?   UNCLE FRED: That's right.

MRS. BOYLE *(Starting to exit)*: I know everyone in a five-mile radius.

AUNT DOROTHY: Marion, stay here.

UNCLE FRED: Marion—

AUNT DOROTHY: Go with her.

MRS. BOYLE: He's not going to bite me, now stop it, Frederick, if you want to come, come.

(Uncle Fred follows Mrs. Boyle off.)

PETER *(To Rita)*: Are you all right?

(Rita nods.)

Are you sure?

AUNT DOROTHY: Oh, what a fuss. Forget all about it, pretend it never even happened.

PETER: We're okay, thanks.

AUNT DOROTHY: Don't you both look so wonderful, and you notice who he wanted to kiss, not me. Oh, you're going to have such a good time, where is it you're going again now? Marion told me.

(Peter waits for Rita to answer before:)

PETER: Jamaica.

AUNT DOROTHY: That's right. For how long?

PETER: Two weeks.

AUNT DOROTHY: Oh, they loved it there last year . . . Your mom and dad . . . Well, I'm going to leave you two alone. Do you want another glass of champagne while I'm at the bar?

PETER: No, thanks.

AUNT DOROTHY: No? . . . *(She moves off)*

PETER: That was so weird, wasn't it? Calling me "honey"? He just seemed so vulnerable. I swear I've never seen him before . . . You're okay?

(Rita nods.)

You sure? You seem . . . kind of . . . Okay.

(The others begin to filter back in.)

TAYLOR *(Overlapping)*: Unbelievable.

AUNT DOROTHY: What happened?

TAYLOR: Just took off down the street, kept going.

DR. BOYLE *(Overlapping)*: Everything's fine now, it's all under control.

TAYLOR *(To Peter)*: Guess he thought you were both kind of cute, huh? . . .

MRS. BOYLE: Oh, my poor babies, to spoil your whole wedding.

AUNT DOROTHY: Have some champagne, Marion.

MRS. BOYLE: No, my god, I'll throw up all those strawberries. *(To Rita)* Your father thinks that's the Evans' gardener, but I don't think it is, do you? . . .

DR. BOYLE *(Overlapping)*: Enough, Marion.

MRS. BOYLE: That's not the Evans' gardener, is it? . . . Rita?

(All eyes on Rita; she turns to look over her shoulder before turning back and smiling.)

RITA: Must have been my kiss is all.

AUNT DOROTHY: That's right.

DR. BOYLE *(Overlapping Uncle Fred)*: That's right.

UNCLE FRED *(Overlapping Dr. Boyle)*: There you go.

RITA: Drives the men wild.

UNCLE FRED: Hear, hear!

TAYLOR *(Overlapping Dr. Boyle)*: This is a party, come on!

DR. BOYLE *(Overlapping Taylor)*: Come on, give me a kiss.

MINISTER: A toast!

AUNT DOROTHY *(Overlapping Taylor)*: Here's to the lucky couple!

TAYLOR *(Singing, overlapping Aunt Dorothy)*:
Celebrate, celebrate!
Dance to the music!

UNCLE FRED *(Overlapping Minister)*: Hear, hear!

MINISTER *(Overlapping Uncle Fred)*: To the lucky couple!

(Someone starts to sing "For They're a Jolly Good Couple!" Everyone joins in, then singing fades.)

PETER *(To us, as he strips down to bathing trunks)*: And there was a toast to us and to love and to Jamaica and to our plane flight and to airline safety and to the old drunk, whoever he was. Whoever he was. I was completely trashed by the time the limo pulled up to take us to the airport. Dr. Boyle told us to sign anything we wanted onto the hotel bill, his treat, and off we went . . . The whole way down on the plane and straight through that first night in the hotel, Rita slept like a baby. I couldn't. For some reason. I kept hearing that poor old guy calling me "honey." "Honey, it's me." Who's "me"? And I'd wanted to protect him. *(Pause)* In the morning we headed down to the pool, husband and wife.

(Jamaica. Poolside. The Jamaican Waiter stands beside Peter and Rita, both in chaise longues. Peter holds a drink in a coconut shell, decorated with a paper umbrella.)

PETER *(To Rita)*: Don't you want to try one?

RITA *(To the Waiter)*: Just a seltzer water.

PETER: Okay. *(To the Waiter)* I'll take another, thanks.

(The Waiter retreats. Beat. Peter notices something on Rita's wrist.)

What's that?

RITA: You like?

PETER: Well . . . sure, where'd you get it?

RITA: Just now.

PETER: In the shop? Here? It's not gold, is it?

RITA: Fourteen-carat.

PETER: You're kidding. How much was it?

RITA: Fifteen hundred or so.

PETER: Dollars?

RITA: Why? He said to charge anything.

PETER: You charged fifteen hundred dollars on your dad's bill?

RITA: I like it.

PETER: Well . . . You do? It's sort of like a . . . it's like a charm bracelet, isn't it?

RITA: It is a charm bracelet.

PETER: Like old women wear? I'm sorry. Look, if you like it, I think it's great. And he did say . . . You're right, he's your dad.

RITA: Relax, we're on vacation.

PETER: I know.

RITA: And you're my puppy-puppy.

PETER: Your puppy-puppy?

RITA: And the world is a wonderful place to live, admit it! . . . *(Handing him sunscreen)* Do my back?

(He takes the sunscreen, looks at it before applying it.)

PETER: Twenty-five? . . . I keep thinking about that crazy old schmuck from the wedding.

RITA: Mmmm, that feels good, darling!

PETER: Who do you suppose he was?

RITA: Hm?

PETER: The old guy.

RITA: Oh, I don't know . . . My fairy godfather come to sprinkle the fairy dust on us.

PETER: Aren't you curious?

RITA: Nope. Come for a swim.

PETER: You just put the stuff on.

RITA: I know. Come on, I'll race you! *(She runs off)*

PETER *(To us)*: Our first full day being married and she seemed like a different Rita. I told myself, It's the excitement. And, come on, it's the rest of your life, you want it to be wonderful. It's natural to ask, "Is this the right person for me? Am I the right person for her? . . . Who the hell is she, anyway?"

(Rita returns, dripping wet.)

RITA: Oh, I love it here, don't you? *(Singing as she dries herself)* "Yellow bird, so high in banana tree . . ."

PETER: Are you sorry you married me? . . . Rita, you were supposed to laugh.

RITA: Oh, shut up.

PETER: Okay.

RITA: I want to go jet-skiing and I want to go scuba diving and I want to go up into the mountains and see the monkeys, okay? And maybe go to a soccer game? *(She plants a noisy kiss on him)* With you on my arm.

(Beat.)

PETER: Do you ever think how we're each a whole, separate being beside one another. Each with a heart pumping inside and a soul and all our memories. How I can never, no matter how close we ever become, share your past, be with you as a nine-year-old, as a baby.

RITA: Don't worry about it, all right?

PETER: I wasn't.

RITA: Just take things as they come and enjoy them. That's what life's for.

PETER: You're right. You're absolutely right.

(Pause. Rita catches Peter staring at her.)

RITA: Feast away!

PETER: All right, I wasn't going to bring this up, but . . . Now just hear me out first; I know what you're going to say, but . . . Okay. You know how you never get any time to work on your portfolio and—well, now that we have just the one rent, what if—just for a while, not forever— you quit tending bar and let me support you.

RITA: Sure.

PETER: What? You'd consider it?

RITA: Why not?

PETER: Really?

RITA: Let you bring home the bacon for a while. Right?

PETER: Right.

RITA: If it'd make you happy.

PETER: Baby, I'm sorry, I'm freaking out. Are you sorry you married me?

RITA: No. *(Remembering)* Oh. Ha-ha-ha.

PETER: I'm serious this time.

RITA: Don't be a silly.

PETER: Okay. Okay. *(To us)* Not okay. The days went by. We went to the soccer game, we windsurfed, or windfell, we ate, we snorkeled, we walked on the beach, always under a ton of sunscreen. And Rita was tireless. Fearless. And sleeping, not that there was anything wrong with that. No, no. Nothing was wrong—exactly. But nothing felt . . . nothing felt. *(Pause)* About a week into the vacation . . .

(Rita and Peter are by the pool. The Waiter stands beside them.)

WAITER: Something from the bar?

RITA: Another seltzer, please, and clean this up, would you, it's drawing flies.

PETER: Oh, I'll have a Long Island Ice Tea this time, thanks.

(The Waiter moves off.)

Doesn't it ever bother you sometimes, though? The black/white thing? I mean, it's so obviously a class issue here, not that it isn't in New York. But you'd think they'd all just rise up and kill us all poolside.

RITA: Why is that?

PETER: Because. We have the money and they don't.

RITA: We worked for it, didn't we?

PETER: Well, your father worked for it, in this case. But, I mean, you talk about the world being so precarious, everything ending in a blinding flash; it would seem a little less likely if things were a little more egalitarian, wouldn't it? If there were a slightly more equal distribution of the wealth, that's all.

RITA: You want to give 'em your money, go ahead.

PETER: No, I . . . Why would you—?

RITA: Peter, you're doing it again.

PETER: I know.

RITA: You take a perfect situation and you pee all over it. Be happy.

PETER: Okay, I was just referring to the people we saw living in abandoned cars and refrigerators out by the airport.

RITA: That was terrible. But you don't have to look at it, do you?

PETER: Oh, good attitude . . . Look, I'm just trying to make conversation, Rita, you're the Commie in the woodpile, not me.

(Beat.)

RITA: Whatcha reading?

PETER: The case histories? Freud.

RITA: Oh. Sounds interesting. Can I read it when you're through?

(Peter stares at her. The Waiter returns.)

WAITER: I'm sorry, sir, the bartender say he don't know what that is.

PETER: A Long Island Ice Tea? *(To Rita)* What goes into one? . . . Rita? An Ice Tea? How do you make it?

RITA: I'm sorry, darling, I've forgotten.

PETER: What, do you have it all written down behind the bar or something?

RITA: I'm on vacation.

PETER: So you can't remember a drink recipe for something I'd like to order?

RITA *(Overlapping)*: Yes. That's right. On the money. Bingo! It's a real busman's holiday with you around, you know? You could fuck up a wet dream!

(She walks off. Beat.)

PETER *(To the Waiter)*: Nothing right now, thanks. *(To us)* It's one thing to forget a drink recipe or a book you read a long time ago, maybe, maybe, but your ideals? It was as if she had switched channels, switched . . . something. *(Pause)* Our last night we walked out on the beach in a light mist . . . like cloth being pulled across your skin.

(Scene changes to the beach. Rita and Peter walk.)

RITA: Oh, it's so beautiful, isn't it? It's great to be alive. And young. There will never be a more perfect night. Or a better chance for two people to love each other. If they don't try so hard. *(Beat)* I remembered the recipe for Long Island Ice Tea. White rum, vodka—

PETER: You don't have to prove anything to me, Rita. *(Pause)* You know . . . I was thinking about you growing up. What—like, what was it like having a surgeon for a father?

RITA: Oh . . . well, it was nice. I always thought, He helps people.

PETER: What about your brothers and sisters? How did they feel about it?

RITA: You'd have to ask them.

PETER *(To us)*: Nobody's memory is that bad! Or was she toying with me? That wasn't like her at all. Unless something was terribly, terribly wrong.

RITA: Peter? Make love to me.

PETER: Here?

RITA: No one'll see. I want to have your baby . . . I want your baby inside me.

PETER: You don't know how that makes me feel.

RITA: Yes I do.

PETER: You don't want babies, don't you remember? You've read Freud's case histories and your father's a dentist, not a surgeon. You don't have brothers and sisters.

RITA: Why are you telling me all this? . . .

PETER: What, you were teasing me?

RITA: Of course I was teasing you. Did you think I didn't know those things? . . . Sweetie?

PETER: You never call me that or "puppy-puppy," you never say: "Don't be a silly" or "Bring home the bacon" or pull the skin off your chicken. You're not drinking, you're not using salt, Rita, you're suddenly—

RITA: I want to have your baby. I'm taking better care of myself. Now, please, darling, relax. You're having some kind of a—

PETER: No. No! You're a Communist, Rita, or Socialist, Democrat, whatever you are, you don't defend the social order in Jamaica or anywhere, you have . . . You're just not . . . You're not . . . you. It's like you don't even need me anymore.

RITA: You need to take a hot bath and look at the moon and breathe life in.

PETER: Rita is afraid of life, she doesn't drink it in.

RITA: I'm going to insist that you see someone as soon as we get back to New York.

PETER: *Je hebt erg witte tanden.*

RITA: Thanks.

PETER: What did I say?

RITA: You said my teeth are white, you know what you said.

PETER *(Embracing her)*: Yes! Thank you. My baby. What do you say?

RITA: What do you mean?

PETER: What's your line? What do you say? Your line, you memorized it.

RITA: I'm sorry, Peter—

PETER *(Overlapping)*: In Dutch! Rita, what do you say?

RITA: I say good night.

(She turns, starts to walk off; he grabs her.)

PETER: No, please! Rita!

RITA *(Overlapping)*: Hey! Watch it, pal!

PETER: I want you to be you, Rita, I want you!

RITA: I am me. This is all I am. I'm sorry I can't be whatever you want me to be. This is me. And maybe what you saw wasn't here at all.

(She walks off. Pause. Peter looks at us. The sound of surf breaking. Lights fade.)

Rita, Peter, Dr. Boyle and Mrs. Boyle at the Boyle home.

MRS. BOYLE: Peter!

DR. BOYLE: There they are.

MRS. BOYLE: Don't you both look wonderful.

DR. BOYLE: Not much of a tan here.

PETER: Well, we decided not to age on this trip.

MRS. BOYLE: Well, you both look wonderful.

DR. BOYLE: Rested.

PETER: That's right.

MRS. BOYLE *(To Rita)*: Did you sleep?

(Rita nods.)

Ohhhh.

PETER: Like a baby. Every night straight through.

DR. BOYLE: Well, you're having a good effect on her.

RITA: It's so good to see you both.

MRS. BOYLE: What'll you drink? Beer?

RITA: Nothing for me, thank you, Mom.

DR. BOYLE: Peter?

PETER: Sure, thanks. Rita's quit drinking.

MRS. BOYLE: Ohhh. Really?

DR. BOYLE: Wonderful.

MRS. BOYLE: So now tell us everything.

RITA: It was terrific.

PETER: It was just great and we can't thank you enough.

MRS. BOYLE: How was the weather?

RITA: Perfect.

PETER: Oh, yeah. Really.

DR. BOYLE: Did you get any golf in there?

RITA: That was the one thing we didn't quite get to, I'm afraid.

MRS. BOYLE *(To Peter)*: He's teasing her.

DR. BOYLE: We took Rita for golf lessons every year for I don't know how many years—

MRS. BOYLE: Three.

DR. BOYLE: Or four.

MRS. BOYLE: Three.

DR. BOYLE: Three. Okay.

RITA: Well—

DR. BOYLE *(Overlapping)*: She never got with it.

RITA: Maybe I'll try it again. I'm serious, I might like to.

(Beat.)

MRS. BOYLE: Did you go snorkeling?

RITA: Oh, sure.

PETER: You name it, we tried it. Rita even wanted to go up on one of those kites—that they haul from behind the boats?

MRS. BOYLE: Oh, you're kidding. No!

RITA: Peter was upset by all the poverty, wanted to give them all our money.

(Dr. and Mrs. Boyle turn and stare at Peter.)

PETER: Oh, show them the bracelet you bought, Rita.

(Rita shakes her head.)

RITA: I didn't bring it.

PETER: Ohhh, too bad.

MRS. BOYLE: I want to see.

PETER: It's gold. It's incredible. All these big things hanging down from it, must weigh about a ton . . .

MRS. BOYLE: Sounds expen—

DR. BOYLE *(Overlapping)*: But you know, that's the reality— excuse me—you can't escape it, wherever you go. *(Pause)* Poverty.

MRS. BOYLE: No.

RITA: That's what I told him.

DR. BOYLE: It's reality.

(Pause.)

MRS. BOYLE: Oh, speaking of which, that man from the wedding, Rita—your father told me not to bring it up, but—was not the Evans' gardener. I called up over there after you left for the airport.

DR. BOYLE: All right, enough.

PETER: Who do you think he was, though?

RITA: I told you, I thought he was my fairy godfather.

DR. BOYLE: That's right.

(Pause.)

PETER: Strange.

MRS. BOYLE *(To Rita)*: Well . . . Why don't we let the men talk about whatever it is men talk about and you can help me set the table?

RITA: Great. Fun.

MRS. BOYLE: And I can show you the sketch I did of your father in class. We'll be ready to eat in about fifteen minutes, gents.

PETER: Terrific.

(Rita follows Mrs. Boyle off.)

DR. BOYLE: When do you start work?

PETER: Tomorrow.

DR. BOYLE: You folks gonna have enough room in that apartment of Rita's?

PETER: Oh sure.

DR. BOYLE: Another beer there?

(Peter shakes his head. Beat.)

PETER: Does Rita . . . ? She seem okay to you?

DR. BOYLE: Why, something the matter?

PETER: No. No.

DR. BOYLE: Tell me, for god's sake.

PETER: No. She seems changed a little bit.

DR. BOYLE: Well, you're married now. And you're dealing with a slippery entity there.

PETER: Uh-huh.

DR. BOYLE: She's always had the highest expectations of everybody. Especially herself. But . . . I don't know, in some way she's always been . . . uncertain. Drove her mother and me crazy for a while.

PETER: Yeah, she told me a little bit. Her politics and stuff.

DR. BOYLE: Politics?

PETER: Oh . . . n—

DR. BOYLE *(Overlapping)*: What politics?

PETER: No, no, I was mixing it up with something else . . .

DR. BOYLE: You'll get used to her. She's young. You're both young.

PETER: She gets, you know, really forgetful sometimes.

DR. BOYLE: I know.

PETER: Forgets whole . . .

DR. BOYLE: Years. I'm aware.

PETER: She's given up salt, too.

DR. BOYLE: Oh, she has. I've got to do that.

PETER: And she pulls the skin off her chicken.

DR. BOYLE: Oh. Well, she's way ahead of me. Watching out for her old age already . . .

(Pause.)

PETER: She's thinking of maybe quitting her job at the bar, too, so . . .

DR. BOYLE: She is.

PETER: Yeah. So I can support us.

DR. BOYLE: Outstanding. You must be making her very happy. Congratulations . . .

PETER: Thanks.

(Rita, Dr. Boyle and Mrs. Boyle exit. Scene changes to Peter's office. Taylor enters.)

TAYLOR: Hey!

PETER: Hey!

TAYLOR: No tan.

PETER: No tan.

TAYLOR: We missed you.

PETER: Thanks.

TAYLOR: Welcome back. Listen, Kollegger wants to know what happened to April.

PETER: Oh. The N.I.H. never sent the documents.

TAYLOR: Oh. What do I tell him?

PETER: Tell him the N.I.H. never sent the documents.

TAYLOR *(Overlapping)*: —never sent the documents. I like the angle. *(He starts to leave)*

PETER: Listen, Tay?

TAYLOR: Yeah.

PETER: If you could switch souls with somebody? . . . Like go inside their body and they go inside yours? . . . You know? Switch?

TAYLOR: . . . Yeeaaaaah?

PETER: Do you think it would be possible, if you didn't know someone, to impersonate them, by just being inside them and . . . looking like them?

TAYLOR: Where are they?

PETER: Inside you.

TAYLOR: And you're inside them?

PETER: Right.

TAYLOR: Why would you go inside another person's body if you didn't know them?

PETER: It's conjecture.

TAYLOR: I think I know that, Peter. But wouldn't you do better to pick someone you knew, a particular person you envied—

PETER: Right.

TAYLOR: —or admired so that you could do or be or have the things this other person did or bee'd or had?

PETER: Maybe. Yes.

TAYLOR: Are you Rita now? Is that what you're telling me? You two have merged?

PETER: All right, here's another question. Have you ever . . . This is sort of a bizarre question. Have you ever been having sex with somebody . . . ?

TAYLOR: Nope.

PETER: And they're doing everything, you know, right more or less.

TAYLOR: Oh, right, sex, I remember, go ahead.

PETER: And you just get the feeling that . . . something is wrong? I mean, they pretty much stop doing some of the things they used to do—

TAYLOR: Ohhhh.

PETER: —and only do certain other things now, more . . .

TAYLOR: Right.

PETER: . . . traditional sorts of things.

TAYLOR: Blow jobs, you mean.

PETER: No, I'm not talking about anything specific.

TAYLOR: No one likes to do that.

PETER: Well, that happens not to be strictly the case, but . . .

TAYLOR: No woman has ever enjoyed doing that, I'm just telling you. It's common knowledge.

PETER: You haven't had sex, but you know all about it.

TAYLOR: Hey, you asked me.

PETER: Yes, I know I did.

TAYLOR: I'm just trying to help.

PETER: Thank you. A lot.

TAYLOR: Welcome back.

PETER: Great talking to ya. *(To us)* That night everything was miraculously restored . . .

(Rita and Peter's apartment.)

RITA: Hi.

PETER: Hi.

RITA: How was work?

PETER: Okay.

RITA: It was? . . . Making you a surprise.

PETER: What?

RITA: Guess.

PETER: I can't. What's this?

RITA: Dewar's.

PETER: What, you're back on the sauce? What's the surprise?

(She sniffs the air; he does too.)

Spaetzles?

(Rita smiles.)

You're kidding.

RITA: I'm sure they won't be anywhere near as good as Sophie's, but then I'm not such a cruel mama, either. You want a Molson?

PETER: Sure.

(She goes off; he picks up a book.)

RITA *(From off)*: So, I don't know, I made some calls about taking my portfolio around today, but the whole thing terrifies me . . . *(She returns with his Molson)* And I started reading that, finally.

PETER: *The White Hotel?*

RITA: Cheers.

PETER: Cheers.

RITA: You didn't call the doctor, did you?

PETER: No, I will.

RITA: No, I don't want you to . . . I know things were hard in Jamaica. Maybe it's taken me this time to get used to being married, but . . . I love you, Peter.

(They kiss. He pulls away, holding onto her.)

PETER: You read her journal, didn't you? You figured out how to fix your hair from the pictures in the albums and what to wear, what she drinks . . . Where is she? Please. I won't be angry. You can go back wherever you came from and I won't tell a soul, you don't have to tell me who you are. Just tell me where Rita is and we'll pretend this never took place. *(Pause)* Okay. Play it your way. But I'm on to you.

(Peter walks out.
The Tin Market. The Old Man is seated as Peter enters.)

TOM: Hey, Pete, you're back. How was your honeymoon?

PETER: Good, thanks.

TOM: How's Reet?

PETER: Great.

TOM: Where is she?

PETER: Oh, not feeling too well, actually. Let me have a double vodka on the rocks . . .

TOM: Got your postcard.

PETER: Yeah? *(He sees the Old Man)*

TOM: There you go. It's on the house.

(Peter does not respond.)

Don't mention it. *(To the Old Man)* Dewar's?

(The Old Man nods.)

PETER: Is he a regular?

TOM: Oh, yeah, last couple of weeks or so, I guess. Why? You know him?

(Peter downs his drink as Tom takes a drink to the Old Man. Peter crosses to the Old Man's table.)

PETER: Have we . . . Have we met?

(The Old Man nods.)

Mind if I sit? *(He does)* You were at my wedding, weren't you?

(The Old Man nods. Beat.)

Do I know you?

(The Old Man nods.)

What's my stepmother's name? . . .

OLD MAN *(Unable to remember)*: Uhhh . . .

PETER: What's the movie I said I was going to see the night I left for Europe? . . .

OLD MAN: *The Wild Bunch!*

PETER: *Je hebt erg witte tanden.*

OLD MAN: Not anymore. *(He shows Peter his teeth)*

PETER: What shape's your father's shrapnel scar?

OLD MAN: He thinks it's shaped like a saxophone, but it's not.

PETER: I knew it wasn't you! I knew it. Oh, I knew it! Oh my god, Rita.

(They embrace.)

OLD MAN: Baby.

PETER: Oh . . . *(Beat. He pulls back)* . . . god . . . Maybe we shouldn't . . . Maybe . . . How much do we owe you here, Tom?

TOM: No, man, it's on the house.

PETER: Oh, okay, great. Great. *(To the Old Man)* Okay? *(To Tom)* I'm just gonna walk the old guy down to the subway.

TOM: Okay.

PETER: Good to see you, Tom.

TOM: You, too. Tell Rita I hope she feels better.

PETER: I will. I will. *(To the Old Man)* Come on, let's get out of here.

(Outside. They walk.)

PETER: How are you?

OLD MAN: I've missed you.

PETER: Where have you been?

OLD MAN: Brooklyn. In Borough Park. I stayed with his family. Julius Becker. He had his wallet on him. I didn't know what else to do, where to go; I couldn't call my mother or go to the police. Who would believe me, right?

PETER: Let's head back toward the apartment. Okay?

OLD MAN: They could throw me into an institution or an old folks' home; I didn't even have our keys. I had to pretend to be him until you figured it out. And I knew you would.

PETER: I think this is like one of those dreams where you tell yourself, Just hang on, and we're all gonna wake up. We'll walk in and she'll be there and it's gonna be okay, Rita.

OLD MAN: I just keep thinking there's something I'm forgetting . . . When he leaned in to kiss me I saw this look in his eye, you know? And something . . . I've got to slow down, I'm sorry.

PETER: That's okay.

(They slow their pace.)

OLD MAN: I get short of breath.

PETER: Better?

OLD MAN: What was I saying?

PETER: You get short of breath.

OLD MAN: Before that. Peter, I'm not senile.

PETER: I know, I know.

OLD MAN: I was holding your hand and then I wasn't. I was turned all around. You were over there and I was over there. I thought it was a mirror, that's why I reached out—to steady myself, and instead I saw his hand . . . this hand . . . on me . . . And then everybody was staring at me and my dad was saying I'd had too much to drink and I don't know, I thought I had salmonella.

PETER: Really? That's great.

OLD MAN: I thought if I went along with it, then you'd all come running out after me and say, "It's a joke, come on, Rita, you're going on your honeymoon." And we'd laugh . . . I just kept walking, past all the cars parked for the wedding. I was afraid to look down at my shadow to see if it was true—my reflection in the windows . . . I found this card in his wallet. *(He shows Peter the card)* "In case of emergency, please notify Mr. and Mrs. Jerome Blier." His daughter and her husband. They came and picked me up . . . *(Beat)* So how was our honeymoon?

(Peter does not laugh.)

Oh, come on!

PETER: I'm fine.

OLD MAN: Does he know you know?

PETER: HE? Yeah. He does.

OLD MAN: She. Whatever. He does?

PETER: Yes, I think so.

(They stop walking. They look up at the apartment.)

OLD MAN: Is he there now?

PETER *(Nodding)*: I think maybe you should wait outside in the hall in case he tries to bolt. All right?

OLD MAN: Peter?

PETER: What? . . . I know, come on.

(The apartment. Peter enters. The Old Man stands outside the open door.)

PETER: Rita?

(Dr. Boyle emerges from the bedroom with a suitcase; the Old Man recedes out of sight.)

DR. BOYLE: Peter.

PETER: What's the matter? Where's Rita?

DR. BOYLE: I'm sorry about all this, Peter.

PETER: Did something happen?

DR. BOYLE: You know I am. You know I like you.

PETER: What do you mean you're sorry?

DR. BOYLE: Rita's gone back to New Jersey with her mother, Peter.

PETER: Why?

DR. BOYLE: I think it would be best if you didn't come out to the house or call for a while until she calms down.

PETER: I went for a walk. Calms down?

DR. BOYLE: We brought both cars so I could pick up some of her things. And I'll be out of your way momentarily.

PETER: Wait a minute, Dr. Boyle, I'm . . .

DR. BOYLE: I'm sorry for whatever personal turmoil you're going through, Peter.

PETER: Turmoil? What did she tell you?

DR. BOYLE: If you want me to refer you to somebody . . . Rita says you're suffering from delusions, Peter. And I should tell you she's talking about filing for a divorce or an annulment, whichever would be—

PETER: What? Wait.

DR. BOYLE *(Overlapping, continuous)*: —most appropriate under the circumstances. I'm awfully sorry.

PETER: What circumstances? What sort of delusions did she say I was suffering from?

DR. BOYLE: Rita . . .

PETER: Go on. I want to hear this.

DR. BOYLE: She was hysterical, Peter, when she called us.

PETER: What did she say?

DR. BOYLE: Rita says you're convinced that she's someone else.

PETER: Someone—? What, and you believe that? What does that mean? Dr. Boyle, I went for a walk. We had a— okay, we had a fight. I went out. You and Mrs. Boyle never have fights? We had a difference of opinion.

DR. BOYLE: I practically had to carry her to the car. Are you telling me that nothing else has happened between the two of you? Nothing at all?

PETER: Seriously, Marshall, think about what you're saying. Rita . . . You're—

DR. BOYLE *(Overlapping)*: If you'd seen that girl's face—I'm sorry, I'm just—I'm going to have to defer to my daughter's wishes.

PETER: I can't believe this. You're just going to take her word?

DR. BOYLE: It's a little difficult to believe . . . knowing Rita as I do, son, that this—

PETER: You don't know her.

DR. BOYLE *(Overlapping, continuous)*: —is all about a squabble, a tiff as you say.

PETER *(Overlapping)*: You don't know anything about her, that's the absurd part. You don't know your own flesh and blood.

DR. BOYLE: Well, I'm sure you're right.

(Dr. Boyle starts to leave; Peter halts him.)

PETER: Rita was a Communist, did you know that? That she was in a Communist—Socialist party? And, all right, here's something else you don't know: we didn't go out for a year. We didn't go out for anything like a year; we went out for two months—at that point, six weeks. We haven't known each other six months now! You wouldn't know if she was lying to you, because you don't know her; you only see what you want to see. And she's lying to you now, Dr. Boyle, she may know certain facts—

DR. BOYLE: Let go of my sleeve, please.

PETER *(Continuous)*: —but that's from reading Rita's journals! She doesn't—watch her! Watch the way she sits! Her eyes!

DR. BOYLE: See a doctor, boy, all—

PETER *(Overlapping)*: Rita—watch the way she listens to everything we say, the way she chews for god's sake, it isn't her! Open your eyes!

DR. BOYLE: I'd like to leave now, Peter. *(Beat)* Thank you. *(He goes out)*

PETER: This isn't happening.

(The Old Man returns.)

OLD MAN: He didn't see me.

PETER: Look . . . I like you very much. I'm not equipped for this. I'm sorry. I still like you.

OLD MAN: Like me?

PETER: I'm not . . . I don't feel the same way about you, I'm sorry. I'm not attracted to you.

OLD MAN: What, are you nuts? I don't think that's the issue, Peter, have a seat, come on, you're—

PETER: If I thought that you were really here, Rita . . . What's the name of the guy you went out with in high school? Wait. You told me once—Rita did—but I've forgotten. And if I can't remember, then you can't. The one who wanted to run away.

OLD MAN: John.

PETER: Oh Rita. *(Beat)* It could have been in my unconscious. You know that. You've read Freud. Haven't you?

OLD MAN: You're not imagining me. Or we're both insane . . .

PETER: All right, think. We've got to try to figure out how . . . This just does not happen.

OLD MAN: Tell me about it.

PETER: All right . . . let me see his wallet, please. May I?

(The Old Man hands over the wallet.)

Thank you. Becker? Is he Dutch, do you know?

OLD MAN: Is it a Dutch name?

PETER: You're the one who says you live there, Rita, Jesus!

OLD MAN: Well, they don't speak Dutch. I mean, I can't exactly ask. I'm trying to keep a low profile in case they find out I'm really a girl, okay?

(Peter rifles through the wallet's contents, finds the card.)

PETER: How do you say the daughter's name?

OLD MAN: Blier. Leah and Jerry. Why?

(Peter picks up the phone, starts to dial.)

PETER: How old?

OLD MAN: Old, I don't know, you know. Forty? . . . What are you doing?

(Phone rings. Leah enters, carrying receiver.)

LEAH: Hello?

PETER: Hello, Mrs. Jerome Blier?

LEAH: Yes?

PETER: Hi, my name is Larry . . . White from the Delancey Street Human Resource and Crisis Intervention Center. Is your father a Mr. Julius Becker?

LEAH: Is something wrong?

PETER: No, no, he's right here, Mrs. Blier.

LEAH: He is?

PETER: Yes, he's fine, he's in good hands.

LEAH *(Overlapping)*: What happened, please? Where—?

PETER *(Overlapping)*: Nothing's happened, Mrs. Blier. He apparently walked up to a couple of young gentlemen and, uh, asked them if they knew what city he was in and they were kind enough to call us here at the hot line.

LEAH: I see.

PETER: But your father's here now and he seems to be fine.

LEAH: Where are you, let me write it down. My husband's—

PETER *(Overlapping)*: I'd like to ask you a few questions first if that's all right.

LEAH: My husband's gone to move the car. I'm sorry.

PETER: Where was your father born, Mrs. Blier?

LEAH: Oh, in Amsterdam. Nobody seems to know the exact year.

PETER: And is he on any medications?

LEAH: He's done this before, you know.

PETER: He has.

LEAH: Two weeks ago he disappeared. We had to go and pick him up in New Jersey.

PETER: Was there some reason? Did he know someone there?

LEAH: Not that I'm aware of, no.

PETER: Are you sure?

LEAH: No.

PETER: Is your father suffering from any mental or neurologic disorders, Mrs. Blier?

LEAH: He's been . . . He hasn't been himself since my mother died last fall.

PETER: I see.

LEAH: Then he had to move in with us . . . I'm sorry, is he there now?

PETER: Yes.

LEAH: Could I speak to him, please?

PETER: Well, I'd like to finish filling out my form—

LEAH *(Overlapping)*: I won't be a moment . . . Please.

PETER: All right. Hang on. *(To the Old Man)* Mr. Becker, it's your daughter.

(The Old Man shakes his head vigorously.)

OLD MAN *(Loud, for Leah's benefit)*: Who?

PETER: She'd like to talk to you. Your daughter!

(The Old Man takes the receiver.)

LEAH: Daddy? . . . Daddy?

OLD MAN: Yes?

LEAH: It's Leah. Are you all right?

OLD MAN: I'm fine.

LEAH: Where are you?

OLD MAN: I'm here.

LEAH: Where did you go?

OLD MAN: I didn't go anywhere.

LEAH: Now you stay there.

OLD MAN: I'm not going anywhere.

LEAH: And you do what the man says.

OLD MAN: Oh, stop worrying about it.

LEAH: All right. I love you.

OLD MAN: Don't worry about it.

LEAH: All right, let me talk to the . . .

OLD MAN *(Under, to Peter)*: Here, you talk to her.

(The Old Man hands Peter the phone.)

PETER *(Into the receiver)*: Mrs. Blier?

LEAH: Yes?

PETER: Is there anything about your father's condition, is there any reason why he might—

LEAH: I can't put him in a home! . . .

PETER: No one's suggesting that you put your father in a home, Mrs. Blier, not at all.

LEAH: I'm sorry. I didn't mean to burden you with any of this.

PETER: You're not burdening anyone.

LEAH: We found out he has lung cancer three months ago. And cirrhosis he's had for years. I can't put him away. He doesn't even have a year to live. You know? . . . If you knew the man he used to be. He ran his own stationery store for forty-seven years. *(Beat)* Let me have your address, please.

PETER: I'm going to have to call you back, Mrs. Blier.

LEAH: Well, wait, my husband's just gone to park the car.

PETER *(Overlapping)*: No, I'm sorry, I'm—I will, I'll call you back. *(He hangs up)*

LEAH: Hello? *(She disappears)*
OLD MAN: What? What's the matter? . . . What did she say?
PETER: Nothing.
OLD MAN: Am I sick?
PETER: No.
OLD MAN: This is me, Peter, remember?

(Pause.)

PETER: You have lung cancer. And cirrhosis. She said she thought you had a year to live.

(Pause.)

OLD MAN: Well . . . Am I Dutch, anyway? . . . Okay, first thing, we need a plan. What does he think happened to me? Where does he think I am? Maybe he doesn't think. Maybe it wasn't intentional. Is that possible?
PETER: It was intentional.
OLD MAN: Maybe it's some form of hypnosis. *(Pause)* All right, here's what we know: he wouldn't have called my parents if he was going to disappear. Obviously he wants to be me. Why? . . . Well, who wouldn't? He doesn't know I've found you, so I probably shouldn't go outside in case he's spying on us and Leah will definitely go to the police anyway, so . . . My dad isn't going to leave me alone with you for a while, I know that. Mom's the one who's going to want us back together; she's crazy about you, and she isn't going to want me around the house, and she certainly won't believe what I'm telling her, she never does, so . . . I say that our best bet is try and get her to bring him here. Don't you?
PETER: He'll scream.
OLD MAN: Let him. The last time somebody broke into one of these apartments, they used a blowtorch and nobody even called—I mean, I had a fire in the kitchen once and went screaming out into the hall. Nobody

even opened their doors . . . We'll think of something. *(Pause)* Okay? . . .

(Pause.)

PETER *(To us)*: The next six days were the worst, the strangest of my life. I called in sick. We moved back and forth from room to room. We played cards, I cooked, we watched TV. It was as if we'd been married forever, suddenly, without the sex. At night I could feel the loneliness coming off of both of us like heat. The third day I called her parents; no answer. I tried again later—the same. The next day, same. After dark we went out to the house; not a sign. We used the spare key to get in; a few suitcases missing, according to Rita, that was all. The next night, still nothing. I called Rita's Aunt Dorothy in Cincinnati. She had no idea where they were and wanted to know why I didn't know. I told her Rita and I had split up. She was sorry to hear it. Rita and I, meanwhile, kept up the pleasantries, the old married couple we'd become.

(The apartment. Peter stares at the TV.)

OLD MAN: Something to eat? . . . Maybe I should teach myself to cook now that I've got the time. What do you think?
PETER: Great.
OLD MAN: Who's winning?

(Peter shrugs.)

Who's playing?

(Peter shrugs again.)

Well . . .
PETER: Rita?

OLD MAN: What?

PETER: What if they never come back? . . . What if they're
gone forever?

OLD MAN: Well . . .

PETER: I miss your face.

OLD MAN: Don't think about it.

PETER: How soft it was.

(Pause.)

OLD MAN: I miss it, too.

PETER: Your hair was so great.

OLD MAN: Oh, come on.

PETER: And your little white feet.

OLD MAN: What, you don't like these? *(Pause)* You know . . .
if you think how we're born and we go through all the
struggle of growing up and learning the multiplication
tables and the name for everything, the rules, how not
to get run over, braid your hair, pig latin. Figuring out
how to sneak out of the house late at night. Just all the
ins and outs, the effort, and learning to accept all the
flaws in everybody and everything. And then getting a
job, probably something you don't even like doing for
not enough money, like bartending, and that's if
you're lucky. That's if you're not born in Calcutta or
Ecuador or the U.S. without money. Then there's your
marriage and raising your own kids if . . . you know.
And they're going through the same struggle all over
again, only worse, because somebody's trying to sell
them crack in the first grade by now. And all this time
you're paying taxes and your hair starts to fall out and
you're wearing six pairs of glasses which you can never
find and you can't recognize yourself in the mirror and
your parents die and your friends, again, if you're
lucky, and it's not you first. And if you live long
enough, you finally get to watch everybody die: all
your loved ones, your wife, your husband and your
kids, maybe, and you're totally alone. And as a final

reward for all this . . . you disappear. *(Pause)* No one knows where. *(Pause)* So we might as well have a good time while we're here, don't you think?

PETER: I don't want you to die, Rita.

OLD MAN: I don't want me to die, either. And I'm going to. So are you. Hopefully later and not sooner. But we got to have this. I mean, what a trip! Meeting you and being in love. Falling. It was bitchin' for a while. And okay, so this isn't such a turn-on, I admit. But . . .

PETER: I adore you.

OLD MAN: What? My hearing. No, I'm serious.

PETER: I said I adore you!

OLD MAN: That's what I thought.

PETER: For better or for worse.

OLD MAN: Huh?

PETER: I said: you would have hated Jamaica. Trust me.

(The Old Man rises, crosses to Peter. Peter stands. They face one another for a moment. Peter can't bring himself to kiss the Old Man. The Old Man hands Peter the phone.)

OLD MAN: Try again.

(Peter dials. Phone rings. Mrs. Boyle enters with receiver.)

MRS. BOYLE: Hello?

PETER: Oh, Marion, it's Peter.

MRS. BOYLE: I thought it might be you.

PETER: Where've you been? I've been worried. How's Rita?

MRS. BOYLE: They've just run down to the store; I may have to get off. She's terrible, Peter. We took her to London. She was so shook up, Marshall thought she needed a rest. I don't know, I was tempted to call you from over there, but I didn't, I'm sorry.

PETER: Is she okay?

MRS. BOYLE: What happened between the two of you, Peter? If you don't want to tell me you don't have to.

PETER: No, I do, I just am not sure I know. I said—I guess I must have said something about her not being the same person. And then I lost my temper with Dr. Boyle; I said some things I didn't mean. I was just so surprised to see him here. You know? Did he tell you?

MRS. BOYLE: No, Peter.

PETER: But I would do anything to get Rita back. *(Looking at the Old Man)* I love her with all my heart and soul . . .

MRS. BOYLE: Well, she says that you're unstable and she's sorry she ever met you. I don't know, you don't seem so unstable to me.

PETER: No.

MRS. BOYLE: Maybe I'm being naive.

PETER: No, you're not.

MRS. BOYLE: That's what all unstable people say, Peter . . . I'm teasing you.

PETER: If I could just see her . . .

MRS. BOYLE: You can't come here, Peter. If either of them knew I was talking to you, they'd have me shot at sunrise.

PETER: How's she been? Is she okay?

MRS. BOYLE: Oh, I don't know what her problem is.

PETER: If she wants me to see a psychiatrist . . .

MRS. BOYLE: Well . . .

(The Old Man scribbles something on a pad and hands it to Peter, who reads as he talks.)

PETER: Marion, what if . . . it's just a thought, but what if you told her I was going away on business for a couple of weeks—

MRS. BOYLE: Are you?

PETER: No, wait.

MRS. BOYLE: Oh.

PETER: And you said she could stop by to pick up the rest of her things from storage in the basement, you know, all her old letters and journals from her childhood and all that stuff she's left here, and then when you came by with her I'd be here. And we could talk.

MRS. BOYLE: Oh, I don't know, Peter.

PETER: I have to see her. Even if she won't even speak to me . . . Please.

(Pause.)

MRS. BOYLE: When would you want us?

PETER: Anytime.

MRS. BOYLE: I'm not promising anything.

PETER: I understand . . .

MRS. BOYLE: Monday?

PETER: Monday's great.

MRS. BOYLE: All right, I'll try. That's all I can do.

PETER: I understand. Thank you.

MRS. BOYLE: What time?

PETER: Anytime.

MRS. BOYLE: Noon, say?

PETER: Noon's great. Fine.

MRS. BOYLE: High noon.

PETER: High noon.

MRS. BOYLE: All right.

PETER: Thank you very much . . .

MRS. BOYLE: Peter?

PETER: Yes?

MRS. BOYLE: What you said before about Rita not being the same person?

PETER: Uh-huh? . . .

MRS. BOYLE: They never are, Peter. They're never Rita. They're never Dr. Marshall Boyle, not the way that you think they should be. They're always someone else. They're always changing.

PETER: Uh-huh.

MRS. BOYLE: That's life. That's marriage. They're always growing and shifting and so are you.

PETER: Right.

MRS. BOYLE: She may not be the picture of the woman you thought she was, but that's an image, Peter. That's just a picture. Words.

PETER: I know.

MRS. BOYLE: I'm sure you're not always the prize either.

PETER: No.

MRS. BOYLE: Nobody is. But I know she loves you and misses you.

PETER: I miss her too.

MRS. BOYLE: All right. We'll see you Monday then.

PETER: Thank you, Mom.

MRS. BOYLE: All right.

PETER: Bye.

MRS. BOYLE: Bye now.

(They both hang up. Mrs. Boyle disappears.)

PETER: She'll try.

(Long pause. Peter slowly kneels and kisses the Old Man tenderly on the mouth.
Scene changes to the apartment, the next day. The apartment is empty and dark. Rita and Mrs. Boyle enter, switching on the lights.)

MRS. BOYLE: I don't want you to be angry with me.

RITA: I'm not. Relax.

MRS. BOYLE *(Looking around)*: He keeps it clean.

(Peter enters. Rita does not see him at first.)

RITA: Yeah. He likes things in their proper— *(She sees Peter)* —places.

MRS. BOYLE: Now I want you to talk, Rita, I want you both to talk, that's all. Peter has something he wants to tell you. If after you've heard him out you don't want to stay, then I'll be downstairs in the car. You can do that much, since you took the trouble to marry him. You might actually thank me someday.

PETER: Mom, are you sure I can't get you something to drink?

MRS. BOYLE: No, thank you, Peter. *(To Rita)* This was my idea, by the way.

(Mrs. Boyle goes out. Pause.)

PETER: How've you been? *(He starts maneuvering into a position between Rita and the exit)*

RITA: I'm sorry.

PETER: Why? You're here now.

RITA: I wanted to come, I just . . .

PETER: You did? Really? Well . . . It's been real lonely here without you, Rita.

(The Old Man appears behind Rita; he carries a kitchen knife and a length of rope. Rita does not see him immediately.)

You went to London, your mom says.

(Rita turns and sees the Old Man as Peter grabs Rita from behind.)

Okay. Tie his feet.

(Rita and the Old Man are holding each other's gaze, unable to move.)

Rita! Come on!

RITA: You don't have to do this.

PETER: Tie him!

(Peter takes the rope as Rita and the Old Man continue to stare at one another.)

RITA: This is not necessary, kids.

PETER: Give me the knife.

(Peter still holds onto Rita from behind.)

Give it to me!

(Peter takes the knife in one hand, holds Rita's arm behind her back with the other.)

Now kiss him.

(The Old Man kisses Rita on the mouth. They separate. Peter releases Rita and wields the knife, particularly wary of the Old Man.)

Rita?

OLD MAN: No. It didn't work.

PETER *(To Rita)*: Is it you?

(Rita shakes her head.)

OLD MAN: No!

PETER: Rita?

RITA: I don't know how it happened. I don't know what I did.

PETER *(To Rita)*: I'll kill you, I swear to god.

OLD MAN: Peter.

PETER *(Threatening her with the knife)*: How did you do this? How the hell did you do this?

OLD MAN: Put the knife down, please.

PETER *(To the Old Man)*: I'll take care of this, Rita! It's a trick, don't you know that much?

OLD MAN *(Overlapping)*: He doesn't know. Give it to me. *(He holds out his hand)* Please. Peter.

(Peter looks from one to the other, paralyzed with doubt.)

PETER: Are you here? Rita?

OLD MAN: I'm right here.

PETER: Talk to me if you're here.

OLD MAN: Give me the knife.

PETER: I can't. I'm sorry.

OLD MAN: Then just put it down.

(Slowly, Peter lowers the knife.)

Thank you.

(Beat.)

RITA *(To the Old Man)*: Where'd you go?

PETER: Watch him.

RITA: I couldn't imagine what happened to you.

OLD MAN: Twelve twenty-two Ocean Avenue.

RITA: How is Leah?

OLD MAN: I think she misses you . . . She keeps putting on professional wrestling on the TV and I just sorta sit there, trying to look interested.

RITA: Interested? It's a joke. We laugh at it together.

OLD MAN: She keeps making soup and offering me another cup and another cup.

RITA: Oh, it's full of fat, she doesn't know how else to make it . . . Your mother . . . she isn't serious about the peanut butter and mayonnaise?

OLD MAN: Oh, she made you one? A sandwich?

PETER: Stop this.

OLD MAN: I haven't had one of those since grade school, I forgot all about—did you try it?

PETER: Rita!

OLD MAN: Oh, they're really good . . .

(Beat.)

RITA: I wanted it, that's all. That's all I know. I'm not hiding anything from you; I don't know any more than that. I started out to take a walk. To just try and get as far away from me as I possibly could, I didn't care. I took the first bus I saw at Port Authority: "Englewood Cliffs." It sounded romantic enough.

OLD MAN: Englewood?

RITA: Yeah. I got off at the first street corner; dogs came up to play. And what's this? A wedding. Young people starting a life. I had some champagne, nobody bothered me. What did it matter what I did? I wished to god I were that young bridegroom starting out. Or the bride, for that matter. Look at the shine in those eyes.

OLD MAN: You're kidding. I was freaked from the moment I woke up.

RITA: Yeah?

OLD MAN: I was terrified.

RITA: No, I thought to myself, If I could shine like the light of that girl over there, I'd never take another drink, I'd let my liver hang on another decade, stay out of the sun, eat right. This time I would floss.

OLD MAN: I remember now. It was you. Oh god, it was your eyes shining back. And you kissed me and, let me be over there, please, let me skip to the end of all this hard part. I wanted to be you. For one second of one day, what would it be like to just be. And—

RITA: Yes.

OLD MAN: —not be afraid.

(They begin to overlap one another ever so slightly:)

RITA: If I could just get inside.

OLD MAN: If I could get inside.

RITA: I'll kiss the bride. I'll be the bride.

OLD MAN: My whole life would be behind me.

RITA: My whole life would be ahead of me again. Look at her. The soft arms. The white teeth—

OLD MAN: That smell.

RITA: The sweet smell on her breath.

OLD MAN: A man.

RITA: Not like something rotting coming up from your insides, but soft—

OLD MAN: Like a father.

RITA: Like a baby. And white.

OLD MAN: An old man . . . With nothing—

OLD MAN AND RITA *(Together)*: Nothing to lose. All you've got to do is want it. Bad enough.

(Their eyes lock. The light in the room dims as if the sun outside were obscured by a cloud—a low rumble. Rita is now standing; the Old Man is now seated.)

RITA: My god.

OLD MAN: Like an old suit . . .

PETER: Rita?

OLD MAN: Don't you see? My wife and daughter had a bond. I loved them both so much I wanted to eat them alive.

RITA: I saw their photographs. Your mom. You just wanted them back, the way they were.

OLD MAN: And women cry, you think. It feels good.

RITA: Yes, it does.

OLD MAN: Women make a life inside their body and that life comes out and holds onto them—

RITA: Yes.

OLD MAN: Clings to them, calls them up from school and says, "I'm sick, Ma, come pick me up." That baby is theirs for life. Where are they now? My wife. My mother.

RITA: They're right here.

OLD MAN: To be able to look back from their side of the bed with their eyes. At last. *(To Peter)* And you, my boy. I tried to be patient, I tried to be interested. I called every hotel in Kingston, "What the hell is a Long Island Ice Tea?" You're a sweet kid, no hard feelings, but you're not my type . . .

PETER: Please.

OLD MAN: I don't know . . . The idea of living forever . . . It's not so good. *(Beat)* And those parents of yours you can keep.

RITA: Thank you.

(The Old Man walks to the door, turns back.)

OLD MAN: Do yourselves a favor: floss. *(He goes out)*

PETER: Rita? . . . Oh, Rita . . . Oh my beautiful . . .

RITA: My body. My body.

(He unties her feet.)

PETER: There they are. Look at those. Yes! Your hair.
RITA: I'm here. I'm not afraid.
PETER: I know.
RITA: I'm not afraid.
PETER: Oh, I love you . . . Give me a smile.

(She does.)

Je hebt erg witte tanden. Je hebt erg witte tanden.
RITA: Ohhhhhh, I don't remember what I'm supposed to say, Peter, I know I memorized it.
PETER: *Om je better mee op to eten.*
RITA: You promised you'd tell me. What does it mean?
PETER: The better to eat you with. Oh, Rita. Never to be squandered . . . the miracle of another human being.
RITA: You're the miracle.
PETER: No, you are.
RITA: You.
PETER: You.

(They clasp one another. Music begins to play. Peter lifts Rita and carries her, finally, across the threshold as a vocalist sings: "How my love song gently cries / For the tenderness within your eyes. / My love is a prelude that never dies: / My prelude to a kiss." Lights fade.)

END OF PLAY

MISSING PERSONS

This play is dedicated to Paul C. Berizzi

An earlier version of *Missing Persons* received its premiere at the Production Company (Norman René, Artistic Director; Caren Harder, Managing Director) in New York City on May 31, 1981. It was directed by Norman René; the set design was by John Fallabella, the costume design was by Oleksa, the lighting design was by Debra J. Kletter, the original music was by Marin Perry and the stage manager was Trey Hunt. The cast was as follows:

ADDIE PENCKE	Helen Harrelson
STEVE WINCE	Christopher Marcantel
HAT PENCKE	Richard Backus
YOUNG BOY	Ryan Sperry
TUCKER PENCKE	Daniel Von Bargen
JOAN PENCKE	Margo Skinner
GEMMA CALABRESE	Antonia Rey

Missing Persons opened at the Atlantic Theater Company (Neil Pepe, Artistic Director; Joshua Lehrer, Managing Director) in New York City on January 31, 1995. It was directed by Michael Mayer; the set design was by David Gallo and Lauren Helpern, the costume design was by Laura Cunningham, the lighting design was by Howard Werner, the sound design was by One Dream Sound, the original music was by Jill Jaffe, the dramaturg was Lynn M. Thomson and the stage manager was Casi Russell. The cast was as follows:

ADDIE PENCKE	Mary Beth Peil
STEVE WINCE	John Cameron Mitchell
HAT PENCKE	Todd Weeks
YOUNG BOY	Cameron Boyd
TUCKER PENCKE	Jordan Lage
JOAN PENCKE	Mary McCann
GEMMA CALABRESE	Camryn Manheim

ADDIE PENCKE (pronounced *"Peng*-key"), an independently wealthy, tenured English professor at Swarthmore College, sixty

STEVE WINCE, a checkout boy at the Food Lion, seventeen

HAT PENCKE, Addie's son, a slag salesman, thirty

YOUNG BOY, Hat at eight years of age

TUCKER PENCKE, Addie's husband, thirty-three (the age of his disappearance)

JOAN PENCKE, Hat's wife, an unemployed software consultant, thirty-one

GEMMA CALABRESE (pronounced "Jemma"), their neighbor, recently widowed, thirty-four

NOTE: Tucker and the Young Boy exist in Addie's mind alone. They are frozen in time, and are invisible to all but Addie until late in Act Two when Tucker also materializes for Hat.

Although the narrow corridor appears
So short, the journey took me twenty years.

Each gesture that my habit taught me fell
Down to the boards and made an obstacle.

I paused to watch the fly marks on a shelf,
And found the great obstruction of myself.

I reached the end but, pacing back and forth,
I could not see what reaching it was worth.

In corridors the rooms are undefined:
I groped to feel a handle in the mind.

—THOM GUNN,
"The Nature of an Action"

■ ACT ONE ■

SCENE I

Moonlight slowly suffuses the house. Clearly visible on the sofa is Addie Pencke, prone, her eyes closed, mouth agape. On the landing above her stands the white, marmoreal ghost of a naked male youth; he holds a quill pen over a sheaf of white pages as in the Renaissance statue Poetry. *He has one foot up on the canister of a vacuum cleaner. He moves, turning his head toward Addie, then slowly descends into the room and approaches her as she rolls toward him, opening her eyes, transfixed by his presence. He comes closer still. Addie lifts her hands to him, and he releases the white pages, which flutter down over her; she receives them ecstatically. Then, the statue retreats as darkness folds once more over everything.*

Lights up again to reveal the same room in morning light. On the sofa Addie stirs and slowly opens her eyes; to her astonishment she finds the white pages still scattered over her like fallen leaves. She sits up and tries to read one, then tries to locate her reading glasses, moving aside an empty wine bottle and wineglass. She reads in silence. Hat descends the stairs, stepping over the vacuum cleaner on his way into the bathroom.

HAT *(Barely awake)*: Happy Thanksgiving.
ADDIE: Happy— *(Remembers)* Shit!
HAT: What?

(Addie crosses quickly toward the kitchen as Hat exits into bathroom. She opens the fridge and lifts an enormous frozen block of poultry out of the freezer, setting it down on the counter with a thunk.)

ADDIE: Fuck me blind.

(She flips the switch on the coffee pot which begins brewing, then reenters the living room where she resumes reading. The sound of a toilet flush, then Hat reemerges and descends into the room.)

HAT: What time did you get up? *(Pause)* You . . . ?
ADDIE: Hm?, two or so.
HAT: Everything . . . ?

(She looks at him.)

You're working . . . *(Short pause)* Joanie brought a man home—not a man, a boy, a *dim* bulb verging on the retarded, I swear to god. "I'll let you . . . I mean, at which point . . . ? I mean, just . . . Okay: you're waiting for the guy to bag your groceries . . . Yes? At which precise moment do you deem it to be the appropriate gesture to invite him to stay in your home, to spend Thanksgiving with your ex-in-laws . . . ? If I . . . If I asked her back, she'd just laugh, wouldn't she?

(Addie holds his gaze.)

What are you . . . ? May I? *(He picks up one of the pages)* What is . . . ? These are my poems! Where did you get these?!? Mom! Oh, Christ. What did you, go through my desk?
ADDIE: They were lying all over me just . . .
HAT: Oh, yes. That is so . . . You *snoop*! God! You expect me to believe that . . . ?

ADDIE: They were all over the sofa when I woke up.

HAT: And . . . No, they weren't. And even if they were, did I ask you to read them?

ADDIE: Are they yours? Was I supposed to know that?

HAT: Oh, right. We've always agreed you weren't gonna read them unless I asked!

ADDIE: Was I supposed to stay away from any and all papers strewn on top of me? I thought they might have been mine. They weren't. It was interesting, I read on, I'm sorry.

HAT *(Overlapping)*: You *knew* those were my poems . . . You thought they were interesting?

ADDIE: I only read one.

HAT: Which one?

ADDIE: Well, is it supposed to be a villanelle?

HAT: What do you mean *supposed* to be? Yes! It's . . . What—? . . . It's a villanelle, yes. What did you think? Any impressions?

ADDIE: Well, it has a lot of plosive sounds. I know that's probably intentional—

HAT: Uh-huh, it is.

ADDIE: —but it seems self-conscious.

HAT: . . . Okay.

ADDIE: "Paranormal," "Papa Doc," "doggy bag," "chocka-block," "bigger chaos."

HAT: Okay, I accept that.

ADDIE: I don't think you can rhyme "chaos" with "Laos"; I wouldn't. I asked if it was a villanelle because before you go shattering all the forms, you should try to prove to your reader and to yourself that you're capable of honoring them.

HAT: Fair enough. What else?

ADDIE: Well . . . it would be my suggestion that all this should come out:

HAT: Which?

ADDIE: This business with the light and the wind, it's too general, it has no urgency, the meter even falls apart.

HAT: That's intentional, too, though.

ADDIE: But why would you do that? It simply seems sloppy.

HAT: Okay.

ADDIE: "A clock upon the wall of fate . . ." That doesn't mean anything. Does it?

HAT: You come up against a wall: it's immovable. Fate. You're right, it's hackneyed . . . Is that, I mean, is that all?

ADDIE: I don't know what the final quatrain means. And I've read it twice now. What is "criminal dust"?

HAT: Oh, yeah, you're right.

ADDIE: No, what's it referring to?

HAT: Oh, it's . . . I'm saying, it's like it's so dusty in . . . his, the "I" of the poem's home or mind or in his soul, it's . . . criminal. I guess. I mean, it's up to the reader.

ADDIE: Well, too much is left to the eye of the beholder. Over and over. Look here, this bit with—

HAT: No, I believe you, I do. You're right. You're absolutely . . .

ADDIE: It's not bad for a first draft. It's nothing to be ashamed of.

HAT: It's one of my oldest poems; I've been working on it on and off for over six years.

ADDIE: Well . . .

HAT: It's been rejected by every major and minor journal . . . But thanks.

ADDIE: Elizabeth Bishop worked on some poems for fifteen years before she got them right.

HAT: Elizabeth Bishop was a genius. Elizabeth Bishop's toilet paper was better than this. I'm going for a walk.

ADDIE: What, should I lie? Is that—? And why would you take my word for anything? I'm not a poetry critic, the hell with me!

HAT: Hear hear.

(He exits without a coat, slamming the door. Addie stares after him: the front door glows with a warm, unreal light. From outside, just beyond the door:)

YOUNG BOY *(From off)*: Mom! . . . MOM!

(Addie rises, moves to her desk, pulls out the chair, opens the desk top.)

Mom! . . .

(The Young Boy comes bounding in.)

MOMMMMMMMM!

ADDIE: What?

YOUNG BOY: I NEED YOUR HELP! QUICK!

ADDIE: What?

YOUNG BOY: I can't get these things off, look!

ADDIE: Your gloves?

YOUNG BOY: No, these.

ADDIE: The clips?

YOUNG BOY: Nobody has these. I'm not gonna lose my gloves: I'm eight years old!

ADDIE: Okay. Don't blame me, your father bought them.

YOUNG BOY: I do not know a single, solitary kid who has these kinds of mittens anymore. Except me.

ADDIE: Well, what do you want, *driving gloves?* Hold on. You should have come to me sooner. *(She removes the clips)* Voilà.

YOUNG BOY: Thanks. *(Remembers)* Oh. *(He takes his report card out of his pocket and leaves it on her desk as he hurries out)* Bye!

ADDIE: What's that? Wait . . . *(Picks it up, reads)* A "C"? In *English?*

(Addie turns back to her desk, pulls out a sheaf of papers, and sets them next to the typewriter. As she sits, the cellar door glows with the same warm, unreal light as earlier in the scene; the door swings open, revealing Tucker, holding a sheet of paper.)

TUCKER: You follow your lights. You're true to your *self*. You take your chances. You do what must be done. You say what must be said. People say you're a fool, it's no damn disgrace, because you did what you pleased. You pleased yourself. *(He presents Addie with the page)* Say it's good or I'll kill myself.

ADDIE: Mrs. Bieler called. Her radio's on the fritz, she wants you to take a look . . . *(She reads in silence)*

TUCKER: What? What did you just smile at?

ADDIE: "The V beneath folds of her skirt."

TUCKER: That's good, isn't it?

ADDIE: Maybe in another poem. Yes. It's sexy, but—is that—?

(Tucker snatches the paper from her and heads back toward the cellar.)

TUCKER: Never mind, you're right, you're a vicious task-master, but you've got exquisite taste.

(He is gone. Beat. Addie turns once again to her desk, hits the first key on the typewriter; then Joan appears above; she descends the stairs, stepping over the vacuum. She is carrying a handful of men's clothes.)

JOAN: Mom? *(Instantly corrects herself)* Addie? Are you—? Is—?

(In frustration at her shattered concentration, Addie rises and moves into the kitchen to fill her coffee cup; Joan follows.)

Did you see anyone around just now?

ADDIE: Hat.

JOAN: You were in bed so early last night, you feel okay?

ADDIE: I wanted to read and be quiet is all.

JOAN: I should have done that. But I didn't. Listen, I thought I was supposed to shop, I thought that's why you left the list on the counter yesterday.

ADDIE: Did you buy a turkey?

JOAN: No. That wasn't on the list. Why? Anyway— *(She sees the cup of coffee in Addie's hands)* No, thanks, that's so sweet. The boy who helped me take all the duplicate groceries out to the car seemed very glum, so I said, you know, cheer up, it's Thanksgiving, to be friendly, that's all, and he said he didn't really have anywhere to go, his family had thrown him out and he was totally broke, and, I mean, I thought that was sad, but I wasn't going to do anything or offer anything except he started to cry which boys that age don't usually do, not in front of strangers anyway, so I thought it was at least a sign of, you know, genuine . . .

ADDIE *(Returns to her desk, sits)*: Psychosis.

JOAN: Well, I didn't even think about that. But he's gone now! I guess . . . He probably put on something of Hat's and hitched a ride back to the Food Lion, don't you think?

(Joan gathers up all the groceries and the handful of clothing. Addie is studying a page of her manuscript.)

Everything okay?

(A beat. Addie looks up. A silent "Mmm.")

Everything okay?

ADDIE: Is it?

JOAN: Is it?

ADDIE: Is it?

JOAN: Is it?

ADDIE: You're both idiots.

JOAN: Who?

(Addie's focus returns to her work.)

Mom—I'm sorry, but I want to take these back before they close—

ADDIE: Be my guest.

JOAN: Why are we idiots? I mean, you drop that into the middle of conversation like—"Everything all right?" "Sure, great." "Well, *you* certainly are an idiot." I just asked if everything was all right. Is it?

ADDIE: Is it?

JOAN: Bye.

(Joan goes out. Addie starts to type; the cellar door glows and opens, as before, and Tucker is there once again with a sheet of paper.)

TUCKER: You follow your lights, you're true to your *self*—

ADDIE: You did this already.

(He brings her the page; again she reads in silence; Tucker sees something in her expression and snatches it back.)

I didn't say anything. I wasn't finished.

(He exits. Addie resumes typing; Gemma and Hat approach the front door.)

GEMMA *(From off)*: You're gonna get sick. Just try one on: for the size.

(Addie rises, moves at once toward the staircase.)

If you don't like it, you don't have to wear it, it's no skin off my nose—

(Hat enters, followed by Gemma, an enormous trash bag slung over her shoulder.)

HAT: *(Overlapping Gemma slightly.)* Mom? Where was Joan going?

ADDIE *(Ascending)*: The store. Morning, Gemma.

GEMMA *(Deposits the bag on the floor)*: Morning! I did it— finally, went through everything.

ADDIE: Oh good.

HAT: What happened to the retarded boy?

ADDIE: No one knows; Joan took his clothes back to the Food Lion. Is someone going to vacuum?

HAT: His clothes, did you say?

ADDIE *(Continuing up the stairs)*: I have no more information, I'm sorry.

HAT: Well . . . His clothes, though?

(Addie disappears. Hat turns to Gemma.)

Did . . . ?

GEMMA: That's what it sounded like. Retarded boy?

HAT: We have a mentally disabled child staying with us. You want some coffee?

GEMMA: No, thanks.

HAT *(Turns toward kitchen)*: Juice?

(Gemma shakes her head.)

GEMMA: You're taking in boarders?

HAT: Joan's idea of charity.

(Gemma follows Hat into the kitchen, where he pours himself a cup of coffee.)

GEMMA: Well, you know, all right . . . I was thinking as I was going through Hammy's clothes and thinking about you and Joan going through all this—

HAT: Uh-huh?

GEMMA: —and her being out of work, and still being here, and my being, you know . . .

(Hat opens the fridge to get some milk: Joan is inside, wearing a nightgown. She hands him the milk and begins speaking; throughout this scene, when Joan speaks, Gemma's voice drops out, although her mouth continues to move. At no point in this scene does Gemma react to Joan's presence.)

JOAN: You're the most important person in my life, honey: you've taught me everything I know about love, you're kind and gentle and bright and good and I want a divorce, I'm sorry.

(Hat shuts her back inside the refrigerator.)

GEMMA: —you wouldn't have to ask her to leave then until she has a little more money, and we have a whole extra bedroom, a guest bath, and any time you wanted you could come right across the yard, visit your mom, your ex-wife, they'd be here—
HAT: Oh, well, that's, Gemma, you know, very kind—

(He reopens the fridge to return the milk, and there, once again, is Joan.)

JOAN *(Slightly overlapping)*: —kind and gentle and bright and good, and I want—

(He shuts the door on her.)

GEMMA: —could leave! Simple as that.
HAT: That's . . . no, that's very generous, Gemma, thank you. I really couldn't—

(He walks right past her, returning to the living room; Gemma follows.)

GEMMA: Let it percolate, don't say no outright; put the idea away in a drawer, in a closet. You'll be surprised to find it: "What's that?" . . .

(Gemma's mouth continues moving, again silently, as Joan appears in her nightgown from a trap in the floor behind the sofa. Hat instantly begins speaking to Joan as Gemma rummages through the large trash bag, retrieving a coat and several other items.)

HAT: Are you sleeping with someone?

JOAN: No, honey.

HAT: Are you sure?

JOAN: I think I would know.

HAT: Do you want to be?

JOAN: No.

HAT: Well, then, what? What is it? My moods.

JOAN: No.

HAT: Yes! When I'm working, I'm awful, I know I am. I am.

JOAN: Yes, you are, but this isn't about you, this is my own . . .
   struggle.

HAT: Whatever, we can work it out, can't we, for the sake of
   . . . the kids we don't have yet.

(Joan freezes; Gemma holds the coat up to Hat.)

GEMMA: —practically your size!

HAT: He was a foot taller than I am.

GEMMA: I'm talking about in the shoulders. Here. The length
   is easy to—

*(Hat, overlapping Gemma slightly, addresses Joan, who
unfreezes.)*

HAT: How did this happen?

*(Gemma slips Hat into the coat, her mouth moving silently.
During the following, Hat will occasionally smile at Gemma
or nod her way.)*

JOAN: It's not you, honey, it's me. It is, it's all me. This—

HAT *(Overlapping)*: Once you get another job, though, come
   on—

JOAN *(Overlapping him)*: It isn't that.

HAT: But being laid off has got to be hard, and we've gotta
   get out of here, we—

JOAN: It isn't that either.

HAT: No, but, no we shouldn't be living with my mom, and that's why we don't make love as much, I think.

JOAN: No, it isn't.

HAT: It . . . isn't? Then . . . Well . . .

JOAN: I'm not as attracted to you as I used to be. And I didn't want to have to say that, but . . .

GEMMA *(Momentarily audible)*: Very handsome, don't you think?

HAT *(To Joan)*: Why?

JOAN: . . . It's all my fault, it's my problem—

HAT: But—but but then we have to see a therapist—

JOAN: Oh, we tried that.

HAT: Oh, come on, he was a quack. He told you to stand on a chair and repeat over and over, "I am a princess and I should have everything exactly the way I want it." I mean—

(Joan re-freezes. Through the rest of the scene, Joan unfreezes whenever Hat's attention returns to her and freezes once he is drawn back into real time.)

GEMMA: I know you're not in love with me.

(Hat looks at Gemma.)

You heard me. I'm talking about friendship. We've both had love. You saw what I was like after Hammy died. Months and months.

HAT: I know.

GEMMA: Like golf shoes walking 'round and 'round on your face . . . You think, I can't breathe, I'm dying: and you are, too, whole pieces of you. Don't say it's any different for you. I see what you're going through: you look like five miles of bad country road in upstate P.A.

JOAN: Pennsylvania has what is called no-fault divorce. All right?

GEMMA: And we both know that someone who can make you laugh in the midst of any single misery is more valu-

able than a hundred million orgasms. Or equal to . . .
many, many . . . some orgasms.

HAT: Thank you.

GEMMA: You're always saying how much you want kids.
I have three of 'em, ready-made!, all of who happen to
think you hung the moon, Mr. Nobody-Loves-Me.

HAT: They don't even like me, Gemma.

GEMMA: I know them. I know their signs, their body language.
They adore you.

HAT: Then how come they never look at me?

GEMMA: They worship you. You're completely paranoid. It's
called being shy.

JOAN *(Overlapping slightly)*: —what is called no-fault divorce.
All right?

HAT: All right.

GEMMA: All right.

JOAN *(Same intonation, a replay)*: All right?

GEMMA *(Indicates the bag of clothes)*: Just go through these
then. All right?

JOAN *(Again)*: All right?

GEMMA: There's a lot of nice things . . . All right?

JOAN *(Again)*: All right?

HAT: Okay.

GEMMA: And . . . you know, you'd, listen, you'd have your
own room with not just a view: *perspective.* Something
to sleep on. Don't start by objecting. Allow. Permit.
Open up. Receive. Appreciate. *Possible. Way cool.* Pretty
great. You know where to find me. *(She goes out)*

JOAN: All right?

HAT *(Wheeling on her)*: ALL RIGHT, ALL RIGHT! Look,
look, okay, I know you probably want your indepen-
dence and I get in your way and I nag you a lot about
wanting kids—

JOAN: It's not that.

HAT: But I will get used to this, I will definitely get used to
this, but—I'll sleep in one of the guest rooms, I'll sleep
down here—

JOAN: Oh, honey—

HAT *(Overlapping)*: Just stay for a while and we'll get a no-fault whatever the fuck that is—

JOAN: It's—

HAT: —because I can't stop seeing you all of a sudden, I can't, that's like an amputation. People bleed to death. It's . . .

JOAN: Like the insurance. You know?

HAT: Fine.

JOAN: Both parties agree to disagree, and it's much less expensive . . . less combative, more civilized . . . I think anyway.

HAT: Okay. You got it. But you gotta stay here. At least until you figure out why you want it.

JOAN: But why?

HAT: Because that's the deal. That's it. That's my offer, plain—

(Addie enters and descends the staircase.)

ADDIE *(Overlapping him slightly)*: Gemma go?

HAT *(Startled)*: What? She left! All right?

JOAN: All right?

HAT *(Same time, to Addie)*: What do you want?

ADDIE: I don't want anything. I live here. Is that all right with you?

JOAN *(Overlapping Addie, taking Addie's "all right" as a cue to echo her)*: All right?

HAT *(Remains looking at Addie)*: I'm trying to think about something, *please!*

ADDIE: Think, who's stopping you.

(Addie heads for the kitchen. Up from the cellar as before:)

TUCKER: You follow your ligh—

(Addie slams the door in his face. She then sets about preparing food for this evening.)

HAT *(To Joan)*: I know what this is. You think I'm a lousy poet.

JOAN: No.

HAT: You think I'm a failure.

JOAN: You could be a genius, and I wouldn't have the first, faintest clue.

HAT: It's because I'm selling slag for a living, isn't it?

JOAN: Well, that's better than doing it for a hobby.

HAT: Now *see*? That's just the sort of thing I can't go without hearing all of a sudden.

(Addie returns from the kitchen.)

ADDIE: You want to know what I think? . . . I think Joan let you support her all this time, and me too by allowing you both to stay here. And now that her self-image is shot to shit, through no fault of her own—

JOAN: —no-fault divorce. All—

ADDIE *(Cutting her off)*: . . . she needs someone to punish. We're the closest things at hand, especially you.

HAT: Well, that's . . . Yes, but . . . I'm sorry, that's really not helpful, Mom.

ADDIE: Okay.

HAT: I understand—I mean, I know what you mean, but she worked for years. And she's doing the best she can. It's just—

ADDIE: I think it's best I stay out of it. All right?

JOAN: All—

HAT *(Same time, cutting Joan off, still looking at Addie)*: It's life. You know? Some people need to go away to find themselves.

(Tucker emerges from the cellar and hands Addie a new sheet of paper, then heads for the front door.)

TUCKER: Well, I'm off to fix Mrs. Bieler's radio! Sun's out!
(He exits)

HAT: And . . . I know it's hard for you.

ADDIE: It's not hard for me, it's hard for you.

HAT: Okay.

ADDIE: . . . Your father disappeared when I was practically the same age you are now.

(Tucker comes out of the cellar again, hands Addie a sheet of paper and heads for the door with:)

TUCKER: Well, I'm off to fix Mrs. Bieler's radio! Sun's out!
(He exits)
ADDIE: You don't think I know how you feel?
YOUNG BOY *(Off; from above)*: MOM?
ADDIE: What you're going through?

(The Young Boy runs down the stairs.)

YOUNG BOY: Mom?
HAT: Mmmm.
YOUNG BOY: Where's Dad going?
HAT: Is that, I'm sorry, but is that why you went through my things?
YOUNG BOY: Where'd Dad go?

(The Young Boy and Hat are both leaning in toward Addie; their body positions exactly mirror one another.)

HAT: Out of some largesse of empathy for what I'm going through?
ADDIE: I did not— *(She stops herself)*
YOUNG BOY: Where'd Dad go?
ADDIE *(Turns from Hat to the Young Boy, her expression softening)*: Come help me with this.
HAT: Seriously. I'm asking.

(Addie and the Young Boy go into the kitchen; Addie begins rinsing and chopping vegetables.)

ADDIE: Do you want to tell me anything about that "C"?
YOUNG BOY: It's just spelling. Dad says that's what editors are for. He says Faulkner couldn't spell.

ADDIE: Oh, he did. Did he tell you Faulkner was an over-rated drunk? Did he tell you what Faulkner said to his own six-year-old daughter when she asked him to take her to a party? "Nobody remembers Shakes-peare's children." Chop these, please, watch your fingers.

HAT: *(To Joan)* What do you mean you wouldn't have the first, faintest clue?

JOAN: I . . . Oh god . . .

HAT: What?

JOAN: I know I always said I loved poetry and loved your poetry, and I do!, but . . . No. I loved the idea of you . . . I loved that you and your mom were this pic-ture I had about what it meant to be artists, but . . . I don't understand poetry, and I never did. I don't know what it's for. I'm sorry.

HAT: For? It's not for anything. You might as well say, "What is music for?"

JOAN: . . . I don't understand the *point*.

HAT: Of poetry? What are you talking about?

JOAN: I know, I know, but . . .

HAT: All these years?

JOAN: Even if you were out in the open about it, if you weren't so afraid, even if you were published!

HAT: It's "memorable speech," that's what it's for. For—

JOAN: Okay.

HAT: For being memorable. Capturing . . . existence, the welter, stopping time—

JOAN: But, yes, fine . . . memorable for who? Who reads it? Six other poets, two of them from Peru.

HAT: It's true, there isn't a lot of demand, but—

JOAN: It has nothing to do with anything I understand.

HAT: What are you —? JOAN! After—

JOAN *(Overlapping him slightly)*: It seems completely useless and—but even if it didn't, even if it were a thrilling and totally intragull *[sic]* part of our lives—

HAT: Integral.

JOAN: —I couldn't help you with it. Intragull. Intragull.

(Hat cringes.)

When you have a question or want my response, which is every ten seconds: I don't know what to say. You're so terrified of failing or being anything less than perfect, so I just kept saying how much I loved it, and reading all those poems and pretending I loved them too, but all the while thinking, I'm beginning to hate this, it's a prison, and I do, I hate poetry, I hate every word of it now, yours and everybody else's, but once I saw how much you needed me to keep cheering you on, I couldn't tell you. That's all. I'm . . .

(Neither of them can speak.)

YOUNG BOY: One "C" is not exactly the end of the world either.

ADDIE: There it is, that's it, right there!

YOUNG BOY: What?

ADDIE: That's the attitude! *Seeping* into every single corner of our so-called culture, the culture of "So? So????" It's no damn good, but it's all we've got, so we praise it anyway. *(Shouts toward the living room)* Praise!, we all want praise, everybody and everything in a second-rate century! Post-modernism, multicultural poetry slams . . . Hip-hop! Rap! Rap *this*, bud! This butt's for you!

YOUNG BOY: Who crawled up yours, speaking of?

ADDIE: It may not be the end of your world, but it's the end of mine.

JOAN: And . . . I just, I hate to see all the suffering you go through, and the rejection. I mean, three poems in three little magazines you can't even tell your mom appeared. And it all sounds like . . . I mean, okay, even the famous ones, the guys with statues in whatever that church was we saw . . .

HAT: Westminster.

JOAN: What are they all talking about, honey?

ADDIE: How are you going to have standards without criticism?

(Tucker comes out of the cellar, as before, and heads for the front door.)

TUCKER: Well, I'm off to fix Mrs. Bieler's radio . . .
JOAN: I don't get it.
YOUNG BOY: Hey, Dad!
ADDIE: Tucker?

(The Young Boy follows Tucker to the front door.)

JOAN: Any of it.
TUCKER *(As he exits)*: Sun's out!

(The door slams shut in the Young Boy's face, the sound reverberating loudly—amplified.)

ADDIE: *Tucker!?*
YOUNG BOY: Dad?
JOAN: I like John Grisham.
YOUNG BOY: Where's he going?

(Addie cannot answer him.)

JOAN: I want . . .
YOUNG BOY: Mom?
JOAN: I'm sorry, I—
HAT: Don't say any more.
ADDIE: Should you ever get to a place you wouldn't show your own mother what you were working on, you were so afraid of what she might say, you'd have to hold yourself responsible for that, no one else, because I would *never* go through your desk, I would never do such a thing, and no one is to blame for whatever happens to you, not me or your father, no one but you, so if you want to go and marry a complete illiterate who will walk out on you for no discernible reason, that's your decision, too, do you understand?

YOUNG BOY *(Clearly dealing with a fragile mind)*: Absolutely.

HAT: All right—OKAY. But . . . stay for two months then, please? Just—six weeks! Until we can work this out gently. I can't go cold turkey. I just can't.

JOAN: I thought a clean break would be less painful, that's all.

HAT: That's understandable, but it's faulty thinking. It—

JOAN *(Overlapping slightly)*: We're gonna have to mourn it at some point—

HAT: I know.

JOAN *(Overlapping slightly)*: —we're going to have to let it go and grieve, sweetheart. It's a natural process.

HAT: Are you hoping to get your own talk show, is that what that is—? "Let it go and—"

JOAN: *There.* That's the voice. Your mother, the critic.

HAT: Maybe—okay, maybe a divorce is the best thing for us. Maybe we'll rekindle or reinvent whatever it was that kept us going until now . . . or who knows? Maybe it wasn't right. Maybe you're . . .

JOAN: Maybe. I don't know.

HAT: Me either. Who does?

JOAN: Good night.

(Joan goes to kiss Hat on the cheek; he tries to turn the kiss into a passionate one; they struggle for a moment before she manages to disentangle herself, angrily, then vanishes into the bookshelves. Hat stands for a moment in reverie, staring at the books. Addie enters from the kitchen.)

ADDIE: You want to help in here? I could use a hand with the stuffing.

(Hat shakes his head no.)

You sure? I'm behind.

HAT: Maybe later.

YOUNG BOY: I'll help.

(Addie returns to the kitchen.)

I never would've gotten the "C" if I hadn't changed to Advanced English. The teacher thought I was crazy when I said, I have to be in Advanced English, my mother says I have to be!

ADDIE: I did not. All I said—

(Steve, naked but for two oven mitts on his hands, which he uses to cover his groin and butt, enters groggily from the pantry; his eyes are puffy, his hair tousled. He and Addie are each surprised to confront the other.)

Oh.

STEVE: Oh. Oh. Sorry—I'm—Steve Wince. So sorry. I'm— look, I must have been sleepwalking . . . and I really, I apologize—I'll uh . . . Excuse me . . . It's very nice of you to let me stay for the holiday.

(He sees Hat, who has approached the kitchen.)

Hi again. I guess I should get dressed. I uh . . . God . . . So embarrassing. Right? *(To Addie)* Good to . . . meet you. *(He backs out of the kitchen, then moves swiftly across the room, up the stairs and off)*

HAT: That's who she invited over.

YOUNG BOY: Whom.

HAT: She asked if I minded if he stayed. In front of him. You were asleep. Happy Thanksgiving . . . Why do you think she took his things?

STEVE *(Reappears on the landing)*: Um . . . my clothes?

HAT: Ah.

STEVE: Did you see . . . ?

(Hat moves into the living room.)

HAT: Joan took them. Back to the Food Lion. There's some things in the closet up there . . .

(Steve turns to go.)

Did you . . . Steve? Did you by any chance go rifling through the drawers of my desk and find some papers?

STEVE: Oh. Probably.

HAT: Probably?

STEVE: Yeah. I like always you know, often, go through stuff, move stuff.

HAT: You do?

STEVE: Especially appliances. Who knows? Right? One day I woke up my arms were killing me, I couldn't figure out what was wrong. Walked in the living room and there was the piano, a baby grand, over on the other side of the room. They sent me to this doctor, said it would go away if I changed my diet.

HAT: Did it?

STEVE: I didn't change my diet.

(Steve exits. Hat remains in the living room.)

ADDIE: This turkey will never thaw.

YOUNG BOY: Why don't you put it in the oven on low?

ADDIE: When you do that, the outside dries and the inside never quite cooks, there's always some ice, bloody ice, right in the middle, like the heart of some evil salmonella snow queen.

YOUNG BOY: I didn't know that.

ADDIE: You didn't? You're a good kid. How about that? Did you know that?

SCENE 2

Evening. Hat and Joan are playing chess. Hat has a tall glass of scotch.

JOAN: The papers came, did you see them? . . . Honey?

(Hat stares at the chessboard.)

I left them for you. I put them on your desk.

(Pause.)

HAT: Do you suppose Steve's parents know something we don't? I mean, do you think maybe he decapitated their little puppy dog and stuck its head on a pole under the porch, and they said to him, "We are frightened, get out, now. And whatever happened to your little friend Mikey anyway, whose face is on all those milk cartons? And how did you come to own his Davey Crockett cap?"

(During this, the toilet flushes, then Steve comes out of the bathroom and descends the stairs.)

STEVE: Did the dinger ding?

JOAN: No.

(Pause. Steve stands over the chess game.)

STEVE: You know, all this time I worked at the Food Lion . . . I know nothing about food. Isn't that . . . ? I lived at home my whole life, until . . . well, yesterday . . . and . . . I learned more about cooking in one afternoon here. From Addie. *(Pause)* So . . . she's like . . . ? Did you say she's like a critic?

JOAN: Mm-hm.

STEVE: A food critic?

HAT: She writes about literature. She wrote a book on Ford Maddox Ford and on Eudora Welty, and she's started one on Nadine Gordimer. Have you read any of them? *(Not waiting for a response)* Oh, what a shame, you should, they're great writers, great, great, really, I know you will appreciate their qualities. *(To Joan, as if he has just heard her)* Papers, yes, I did see them, thank you. In time for Thanksgiving they came, so we can include them in our prayers, too, that's good. *(To Steve, without stopping)* She's the head of her department at Swarthmore. She writes book reviews and cultural pieces for the *Sentinel*.

STEVE: That sounds familiar.

HAT: It's your local newspaper.

STEVE: Then that's why.

(Silence. Hat studies the board.)

Well . . . I'd better . . . 'Scuse me . . .

(Steve moves into the kitchen and resumes cooking. Joan studies the board.)

HAT: Explain to me, just, I mean, I'm sure it hasn't escaped your notice that he is dressed entirely head to toe in my clothes as if impersonating *me*. In my house.

JOAN: Steve?

HAT: Was there a reason you took his clothes back to . . . ?

STEVE *(Same time as Hat)*: Yeah?

JOAN *(Also through Hat's line)*: Would you mind taking those clothes off?, and putting on some of these from this bag?

STEVE: Oh, I thought you wanted me to strip.

HAT: That's okay, really.

JOAN: They have a very symbolic value. They belong to someone who used to live here.

STEVE: Oh.

JOAN: Someone we were all very fond of once a long *long* time ago, but something here will fit you, I'm sure.

HAT: It isn't necessary, really.

STEVE: I didn't know about the dead guy, I thought they were yours.

JOAN *(Picking through clothes)*: Oh, he isn't dead, per se, no, spiritually maybe; that's the funny thing, though, see: it's *possible* he was just a figment of all the things I thought I needed, but didn't really—which would be a big relief. Here, this looks like a good combo.

STEVE: I'm real sorry.

JOAN: That's okay.

STEVE: I didn't know. They were hanging in the closet.

JOAN: That was our room. Together.

STEVE: Yeah, well, listen, it's none of my business. I should have . . . kept mine on, right?! I'll hang these back up. *(Indicates the new clothes)* Whose are these, though?

JOAN: Hammy's.

STEVE: He won't mind?

JOAN: He won't mind.

(Steve goes up the stairs and off. Joan sits back down, staring at the chessboard, fuming.)

The whole fucking world is gonna have to leave you before you deal with anything . . . Isn't it? . . . Isn't it?

(Pause.)

HAT: To have actually been present when Joan's Theory was born, it's kind of—

JOAN: Your *soul* is sick, Hat, and you can't even see it.

HAT: I love it when you quote Kahlil Gibran.

JOAN *(Tiny beat before)*: At least he got his poems published.

(Silence. Joan moves a chess piece.)

Check. *(Stands)* You think, you and your mom, that you are so genetically superior, but what is it that makes you so?

(Steve starts down the landing and freezes like a deer caught in headlights when he hears:)

What? What? YOU STUPID FUCKING FAT FUCK-FACE!

(The kitchen timer begins to ding. Joan turns and heads for the bathroom, slamming the door behind her. Hat looks at Steve.)

STEVE: The . . . the dinger, excuse me.

(Steve starts down the stairs; the front door swings open, and there is Addie holding two pies in front of her face.)

ADDIE: What am I? What am I? Go ahead!
HAT: I don't know, what are you?
ADDIE: I'm pie-eyed, what do you think?

(Gemma and the Young Boy follow Addie into the living room; the Young Boy remains invisible to all but Addie.)

GEMMA *(To Steve)*: Hello.
ADDIE: Steve, Gemma.
STEVE: How do you do?
GEMMA: A pleasure.
ADDIE: The pies came out beautifully, Steve.
STEVE: Oh good.
ADDIE: And we are going to eat one now while we wait for that endless fucking turkey.
HAT: Why don't you wait until after the meal?
ADDIE: Why don't you mind your own business, buster?
HAT: Great.

(Steve follows Addie and the Young Boy into the kitchen. Joan comes out of the bathroom.)

ADDIE: Any end in sight?
STEVE: Well . . .
ADDIE: Well, it'll finish in time for my memorial service. You can eat it and think of me: take, eat, this is my body.
JOAN *(To Gemma)*: Where are the girls?
GEMMA: Oh, they wanted to wait until the food was ready.
ADDIE: No, they don't want to come!
GEMMA: Yes, they do.
ADDIE *(In doorway between kitchen and living room)*: It's their first Thanksgiving without their father, they want to stay home. And who can blame them? Who wants pie?

GEMMA: Me!

JOAN: No, thank you.

HAT: No, thanks.

STEVE: Sure.

GEMMA: They were playing Candy Land. Except for Debbie. She was staring out the window the way she does—like a zombie.

JOAN: Well . . . she's a teenager.

GEMMA: I don't know what she is. But . . . she's mine, that's for sure!

ADDIE: Just leave all that, Steve, and come nibble.

STEVE: Well, I'm almost finished here with the creamed onions. I'll be in.

ADDIE: You are an angel from heaven. *(To the Young Boy)* So are you! Come on.

(She carries three slices of pie into the living room, the Young Boy close on her heels.)

GEMMA: Doesn't this look good. She's started pulling out her hair, too, though, one by one.

JOAN: Debbie?

GEMMA: She's almost bald.

JOAN: I thought her hair looked a little thin.

GEMMA: I'm gonna have to buy her a wig. Or take her around the world until she stops and it grows back. Why don't you travel, Addie, you and me and Debbie, with some of your dough, huh?

ADDIE: Me? What dough?

(Addie and the Young Boy sit on the sofa. She pats the space beside her for the Young Boy to move closer to her; she puts her arm around him and strokes his head.)

GEMMA: Come on. Isn't there any place you ever wanted to see?

ADDIE: We traveled when I was little. I hated it.

GEMMA: The trust fund kid here.

(Addie gives her a look.)

I'm sorry. Ever since I got the money from Hammy's insurance, it's all I can think about. I'm rich! And I can't believe it, I can't enjoy it.

ADDIE: Yes, you can.

GEMMA: Then let's travel together—goombahs.

ADDIE *(Overlapping slightly)*: No, no.

JOAN *(Rising)*: Anybody want anything to drink?

ADDIE: Me.

GEMMA: Me, too.

(Joan goes into the kitchen and pours herself a very tall glass of wine and knocks it back before filling three normal-sized glasses.)

Why not? Why shouldn't we see the world?

ADDIE: Because. I hate travel. The last time I flew on a plane I realized why.

GEMMA: Why?

ADDIE: You have to meet other people. You have to listen to all their noise. There's no quiet place in an airport. Did you ever try to read in one of their "lounges" quote-unquote? Blaring endless Muzak as if we were all trapped in some hellish game show. The entire structure of America is designed to keep people from being quiet and thinking about their lives.

GEMMA: Well, who would want to do that?

JOAN: Steve? Some wine?

STEVE: Sure.

ADDIE: And all those congenital idiots who don't know that their tray table banging up and down is attached to the back of the seat of someone in front of them, so every time they change their mind and smash it up or bang it back down they are smashing and banging the seat of a person, and if you gently request that they stop that, they look at you like you've just asked them to swallow your fart and hold onto it for safekeeping.

JOAN *(To Steve)*: Good work in here!

(Joan gives Steve a little congratulatory peck on the cheek; this registers with him powerfully, however.)

ADDIE: And then the imbecility of applauding a safe landing as if we were a truckload of Albanian peasants. No, no, no. And people who exit the plane and stand right there in front of you at the end of the ramp as if they were the last people on earth. No wonder we're despised from one hemisphere to the next.

JOAN *(Returning with the glasses of wine)*: Cheers, everybody, happy Thanksgiving.

GEMMA AND STEVE: Cheers.

YOUNG BOY *(Toasts an invisible glass)*: Cheers!

GEMMA: I agree. Let's stay home.

HAT: To home! No place like it.

GEMMA: Home!

(They all drink except for Addie, who stares at Hat drinking his drink. He smacks his lips in mock appreciation, then says:)

HAT: Ah, cha-cha-cha-cha!

ADDIE: To think that little *snerk* came out of my body.

YOUNG BOY: Remember that part in *Nicholas Nickleby*? "You are my home!" You are. *(He puts his arms around Addie)*

ADDIE: Thank you.

GEMMA: Delicious.

HAT *(To Joan)*: Are we gonna finish our game?

(Joan does not respond; Steve moves into the room.)

GEMMA *(To Steve)*: Everything smells so good. Addie tells me you've been helping in the kitchen.

STEVE: Well, I mean, it's fun.

GEMMA: I'm sure it is.

STEVE: I load people's groceries all day long and I never really thought about how they're gonna go home and cook.

GEMMA: Aw.

STEVE: I always, I don't know, I always thought . . . just on some . . . weird level, you know, like I would like to be a chef.

GEMMA: Uh-huh?

STEVE: But I never met anybody who knew anything about cooking. It's great to just, like, you know, learn something new—

GEMMA: Uh-huh?

STEVE: . . . a whole new . . .

GEMMA: Yes, it is! Isn't it!

STEVE: . . . It's . . . well . . . I like it.

GEMMA: Now, tell me, do you live in a group home, is that right?

STEVE: No, my—I mean, my mom lives right in town.

GEMMA: Oh, you live with your mom. Isn't that great? You have a big vocabulary, too. You do. I just think it's wonderful that you can learn a vocation like helping people bag their groceries and now cooking; the world is pretty much your oyster, isn't it?

STEVE: Yeah. Sort of.

ADDIE: Gemma, Steve is fully competent.

GEMMA: Well, of course he is. My goodness. And we're very very glad to have him with us. Now my youngest one? Don't tell her I told you . . . She broke her two teeth up here.

STEVE: Oh. When?

GEMMA: Yesterday. Trying to walk on her lips, she said. Life is strange. They need a father. *(Short pause. To Joan)* Joan, tell me, how'd you ever get yourself hooked up with a poet?, I want to know.

JOAN: Oh, I don't know. Opposites attract, I guess.

GEMMA: You have such beautiful hair. You don't look at all like a computer programmer.

JOAN: Well, what does that look like?

GEMMA: I don't know, but . . . doesn't she? Have beautiful hair?

HAT: I think she looks just like one: a glamorous computer programmer.

JOAN: I want to chop it off, but thank you.

GEMMA: Let me know if you do. I'd like to give some of it to Debbie.

(Steve pulls a thin paper volume off one of the bookshelves.)

STEVE: Is this someone related to you? Isn't this your name?

ADDIE: What? Where did you find that?

STEVE: Right here.

ADDIE: Oh my . . . Yes.

HAT: It's my father's only book of poems. It's actually a chapbook.

GEMMA: Let me see.

HAT: That means it's sort of a pre-book book. My mother paid to have it printed.

ADDIE: None of that means the poems aren't good.

HAT: Of course not.

GEMMA: I always forget that he was a poet. I never understand poetry, not that I ever give it much of a shot. *(To Addie, teasingly)* Did you criticize him away? I'll bet you did!

ADDIE: I'm not a poetry critic.

GEMMA: I know. I'm teasing.

ADDIE: Yes . . . Well, I thought it bore repeating.

(Steve and Gemma read a poem in silence. At some point Addie mutters, still marveling at the sheer balls of: "Did you criticize him away?" Then, in the silence, both Addie and the Young Boy watch as Hat's gaze drifts over to Joan. He stares at her longingly. Addie and the Young Boy look at one another, then Addie gives him a gentle push toward Hat.)

YOUNG BOY *(To Hat)*: Say something, man! Convince her! If you want to keep her! Say something eloquent, poetic! Go on! Say it! In front of all these people: "I love you!" Say it! Caution to the winds, asshole!

GEMMA: I'll have to read it again when I'm sober.

YOUNG BOY: You blew it.

STEVE *(Finishes the poem)*: Wow . . .

YOUNG BOY: Christ.

STEVE: But . . .

YOUNG BOY: You deserve to be alone.

STEVE: . . . that's whose clothes I had on before?

(Steve looks at the book jacket to find the name. Hat's gaze remains on Joan.)

Tucker?

ADDIE *(Coming out of her reverie)*: Tucker? No.

STEVE: Oh. *(He looks at Joan for a second)* I thought—

(Gemma suddenly recognizes what Steve is wearing.)

GEMMA: Oh, I was sitting here, thinking, My husband had a shirt just like that! *Someone's* getting some use out of those things at last. Ohhhhh. You hate to give 'em to the Salvation Army, to think of a bunch of strangers wearing all the things you took so much time to pick out. My husband died a year ago, December. Doesn't that look nice on you!

STEVE: Did he live here then?

GEMMA: My husband? No, he lived with me. Goodness.

STEVE: Well, who . . . ?

GEMMA *(To Addie, sotto voce)*: Should he be drinking alcohol?

HAT: Steve, it's understandable that you or anyone would have been confused by what Joan said before.

YOUNG BOY: Oh, yeah, that'll win her back. Nice.

GEMMA *(Takes Steve's wine)*: Let me take this.

YOUNG BOY: Give it up.

GEMMA: My husband was a wonderful man. You would have liked him.

JOAN: Yes, he was.

GEMMA: Everyone liked Hammy.

HAT: Yes, they did.

GEMMA: He had such a gift for life, for making people laugh—
HAT: That he did.
GEMMA: . . . He went down to get the mail and . . .
JOAN: Let's . . . I'd like to propose a toast!
GEMMA: A drunk driver—at 10:30 in the morning.
JOAN: To the chef!
GEMMA: Can you imagine?
JOAN: And to all our loved ones, here and looking down.
GEMMA: He always cried after we made love. He was so happy.
ADDIE: Maybe it was painful for him.

(Gemma looks at Addie, hurt, unsure if she has even heard her correctly.)

It was a joke, a bad one.
GEMMA: I never know when anyone's joking anymore. He was so rational, though, all through it all. I heard the crash and knew. I knew. And when I ran down, he was so calm and levelheaded. "You and the girls are going to be fine. The insurance papers are in the bottom drawer on the right. Call Robert MacGowan, he'll take care of you. The mortgage is insured." So practical. And he covered up a bone sticking out as if he were ashamed of it, you know?
ADDIE: Okay.
GEMMA: Oh, I tell you, Joan, if I had a husband as sweet as this one right here, I wouldn't let him go for all the world. Oooo, I'd hold on tight, I would. But . . . thank god for food, that's all I can say. *(She takes a bite of her pie)*
JOAN: Coffee, anyone?
GEMMA: Some pie, Joan?
JOAN: No, thank you. *(She turns toward the kitchen)*
GEMMA: Oh, go ahead.

(Gemma lobs a piece of pie at Joan, catching her squarely between the shoulder blades.)

You're all skin and bones!

JOAN: Oh.

GEMMA: Well, look at her! —I'm sorry, I'm sorry, I can't drink.

JOAN: It's okay. No harm done.

HAT: Up we go. Come on.

(Hat tries to lift Gemma; Steve helps Joan clean up the pie. The Young Boy is watching, shocked.)

GEMMA: I thought you'd think it was funny. All right, I'm going home. Hat, I'm sorry.

ADDIE: We'll call you when the turkey has been completely fossilized, all right?

GEMMA: Joan, I'm so sorry.

JOAN: It's okay.

GEMMA: Oh, Addie . . . you look awful.

ADDIE: Go home now.

GEMMA: Well, she told me! I'm sorry about the pie.

JOAN: Don't worry about it.

GEMMA: Well, I feel badly.

JOAN: It's all right, it'll come out.

ADDIE: Take some pie to the girls while they wait.

GEMMA: We're still friends?

JOAN: Yes, here, why don't you take the rest of this one back to the girls—

HAT: That's a good idea.

JOAN: —and we'll call when everything's done.

GEMMA: Did I have a coat?

ADDIE AND HAT: No.

GEMMA *(Taking the pie)*: Thank you for this. In my reign as Miss America, I intend to work for all the brain-damaged kids— *(Realizes what she has said vis-à-vis Steve)* For the Bill of Rights. In the coming year I hope to bring light into the dark lives of many. Thank you all for making this a dream come true.

(Hat drapes Gemma in one of Hammy's sweaters.)

Oh! And as a token of my esteem, I'd like to give you all a little something.

HAT: No, Gemma, stop.

GEMMA *(Slinging two more pieces of pie at Joan)*: One for you, and one for you—

HAT: I said stop! Give it to me.

GEMMA: You're all about as much fun as a funeral. Come on, I'm playing.

HAT: I'm gonna take her home.

STEVE: I'll help.

HAT: Say good night, Gemma.

GEMMA: Oh, Hat.

HAT: Come on.

GEMMA: Oh, really! I'm sorry, I'm sorry, I'm sorry. I thought you'd laugh. I thought it was funny. It was funny! Oh, Hat, I'm fine. Come on. Now I'm embarrassed.

(Steve and Hat escort Gemma out. Joan finishes cleaning up the mess.)

JOAN: Should we baste the turkey or something? . . . I'll do it . . . Let's you and me make peace at least.

ADDIE: I didn't know we were at war.

JOAN: You and me? You and I. Oh, the hell with it. I had such a crush on you when Hat and me were in school, Hat and I, I'll never sort it out.

ADDIE: It's okay.

JOAN: I'd never met an adult who read so many books and taught, I mean, outside my teachers . . . Someone who didn't have a TV. I was so impressed.

ADDIE: You impress easily, I suspect.

JOAN: No, I loved you. I do love you . . . I'm sorry about the way things have turned out, you know that.

ADDIE: I don't want to know anything I don't already know. All right?

JOAN: Fair enough.

(Tucker emerges from the cellar, handing Addie a freshly typed poem before exiting with:)

TUCKER: Well, I'm off to fix Mrs. Bieler's radio! Sun's out!

ADDIE: I was going to divorce Tucker once. I ever tell you that?

JOAN: I don't think so. What happened?

ADDIE: He disappeared for twenty-three years, didn't seem much point.

JOAN: You're really very angry at me.

ADDIE: No, I'm not.

(Addie picks up a newspaper. Pause.)

JOAN: Did you ever like me? Do you?

ADDIE: Don't torment an old woman, it's late; I want to read in peace. Of course. Go have some coffee.

(Joan kicks her in the shin.)

Ow!

JOAN: Talk to me!

ADDIE: Did you kick me? What the hell's the matter with you?

JOAN: I didn't mean to kick you that hard, but I want you to connect with me! "Just connect!" You know?

ADDIE: "*Only* connect!"

JOAN: "Only connect."

ADDIE: You . . . This idea that you or Hat or anyone has some inalienable right to your desires.

JOAN: I'm sorry.

ADDIE: It's the pursuit of happiness, it doesn't say anything about getting it. Now leave me be. Please. I request it. As home-owner.

(Joan stands for a moment before turning and starting up the stairs; Addie does not take her eyes off the paper. Tucker then emerges from the cellar, as before, handing Addie a freshly typed sheet of paper and exiting with:)

TUCKER: Well, I'm off to fix Mrs. Bieler's radio. Sun's out!

(Pause. Addie crumples the sheet of paper. Tucker emerges again from the cellar.)

Well, I'm off to fix Mrs. Bieler's radio. Sun's out!

(He exits. Addie crosses to the cellar, locks the door. She returns to her newspaper. The door handle jiggles. Harder. From off:)

Addie? . . . AD? . . . *(He pounds loudly)* ADELAIDE? . . . *'EY!*

ADDIE *(To the Young Boy)*: Go to bed.

YOUNG BOY: But—

(The pounding suddenly stops.)

ADDIE: Now!

YOUNG BOY: It's only seven o'clock.

ADDIE: Do as I say this instant! Do you hear me?

YOUNG BOY: Why?

ADDIE: Because!

(Suddenly something crashes against the cellar door: an ax, chopping through the wood, splinters flying.)

GO! AND LOCK YOUR DOOR!

(The Young Boy charges up the stairs and off; Tucker's hand reaches through the hole in the door and unlocks the latch; the door swings open and Tucker walks smoothly, triumphantly through.)

TUCKER: Well, I'm off to—

(Addie moves to block his path.)

ADDIE: Tucker Pencke, how dare you come in here and frighten us like that, how dare you criticize me?

TUCKER: Criticize?

ADDIE: Did I? Did I criticize you away?

TUCKER: Did you?

ADDIE: How could you stop?

TUCKER: How do you know I did?

ADDIE: Was it just to hurt me? Is that why you quit?

TUCKER: Did I? Is it?

ADDIE: All right, enough.

TUCKER: I'd never have predicted this—this character you've honed. I'd have said, New husband, new worlds—no shrine to the past.

ADDIE: What shrine? Don't flatter yourself.

TUCKER: Where have you looked? Come on, get it out. Say it all.

ADDIE: Oh, you want me to share? Thank you for sharing. You've missed the funniest show on earth, my darling, the devolution of American values. They're crowing now over the collapse of the Soviet Empire, drinking radiation in congratulatory toasts, dancing on their own graves: market capitalism triumphs over life itself.

TUCKER: Where?

ADDIE: Democracy, our precious choice between two parties, Tweedledum and Tweedledumber, pretending to duke it out, distracting by collusion a benumbed mass of cocaine slathering, gun-toting MTV connoisseurs. Laugh, clown, laugh.

TUCKER: How many hospitals you call all told?

ADDIE: Johnny One-Note. *Thirty-two*, but who was counting?

TUCKER: Where else? Where'd you look?—

ADDIE: In print. Knew you'd be pleased.

TUCKER: Was I there?

ADDIE: Were you? If you were using your own name at that point, I knew you must've wallpapered the inside of your trailer with rejection slips, and there was some solace in that. I thought I'd found you for a while in the voice of James Schuyler. There was a chatty, botanical laxness there, just enough talent to get by, never overreaching himself. Oh, there I go . . . But I did catch glimpses of you I thought in Merwin, Lowell, Charlie Williams, even Anne Sexton.

TUCKER: Okay, I admit it. You ever try to picture her without that wig?

ADDIE: Your son took my many subscriptions as an interest in poetry generalis. He's writing at night, has been for years, I'm afraid.

TUCKER: Afraid?

ADDIE: Yes.

TUCKER: Of?

ADDIE: He's good. I think he's good.

TUCKER: Afraid you'll drive him out? Like you did me?

ADDIE: Did I?

TUCKER: Where else?

ADDIE: No, it's enough.

TUCKER: Go on.

ADDIE: I went through four private eyes; flew to Washington to see the opening of the Vietnam Memorial, ran my fingers down the stone . . .

TUCKER: Was I there?

ADDIE: Were you? Any and all lists of accident victims, plane crashes far and wide . . . The Quilt . . . Would, I sometimes wondered, some coffee-colored child approach me in the check-out line? "Mrs. Pencke?" "Yes?" "I'm Tucker's girl. He's in the meat section—now. He can't bear to face you . . . This is my mother, Irene." "Hello, Irene." And I would see all at once everything you hoped for and couldn't find here, in me, so you sent me looking for it too, in clerks and congresswomen, photographs, Thomas Hardy novels, Trollope just now—why am I defending myself to you? Get out.

TUCKER: What else?

ADDIE: Nothing, no more.

TUCKER: Then why are you thinking about me?

ADDIE: I'm not, I'm through thinking about you.

TUCKER: What is it you want?

ADDIE: A card, a call, an obituary—let me off the hook—die, for god's sake. Age! Be! I don't care. A cable from an oil tanker, a Cuban jail; that would be nice, actually, perfect, lost, forever chasing after the ghost of socialism . . . rewarded finally for our noble Stalinist convictions, something, anything.

TUCKER: To know me.

ADDIE: No! Screw that, bury you, if I could, once and for all. *Know* you? Tucker, I wouldn't recognize you if you walked in now and kissed me on the lips.

TUCKER *(Approaching her)*: Would you like that?

ADDIE: I would not. Get away from me, I'm drunk—I haven't brushed my teeth, don't touch me.

TUCKER *(Continues approaching)*: Or? What would happen?

ADDIE *(Overlapping)*: I'll—you son of a . . . No.

(He slowly brings his lips to hers and kisses her.)

Thank you, Tucker.

(He begins unbuttoning her blouse.)

Just once. And you're out. And I mean that.

YOUNG BOY *(From off)*: Mom?

(Music plays as the Young Boy appears on the stairs, watching, as Tucker buries his face in Addie's belly. The Young Boy is fascinated.)

ADDIE: Slow . . . slower . . .

TUCKER *(Stops, looks up at her)*: Critic.

*In the darkness, the sound of a pitch pipe. Lights up on a proces-
sional from the kitchen into the living room: Steve carries the
turkey on an enormous platter, covered; he is accompanied
by Addie, Hat, Joan, the Young Boy, Gemma and Tucker, all
singing "Shall We Gather at the River." They each carry a small
platter of food in one hand—vegetables, salad, cranberry sauce,
etc.—and a candle in the other.*

ALL:

    Shall we gather at the river
    Where bright angel feet have trod;
    With its crystal tide forever
    Flowing from the throne of God?
    Yes, we'll gather at the river
    The beautiful, the beautiful river,
    Gather with the saints at the river
    That flows from the throne of God.

    *(On the final chord, the platters are set down on the coffee
    table, which has been draped with a large white cloth.
    Everyone gathers around, the Young Boy disappearing in
    the tight huddle of adult bodies.)*

HAT: Let us pray. *(He looks to his mother)*
ADDIE: Oh. Me? Not my usual . . . *(Bows her head)* Lord . . .
    we . . . thank you for . . . the great pleasure of your . . .
    not usually at a loss, we thank you for this food which
    we are about to eat . . . And for our guests and our
    beloved family and for . . . the glory of our . . . lan-
    guage, the mysterious treasure of English, we thank
    thee, oh Lord, whoever, wherever you are, amen.
    Phew!
ALL *(Overlapped)*: Amen.
TUCKER: Dig in!
GEMMA: Yes!
JOAN: Let's eat!
HAT: Mmmmm!

*(Tucker hands Addie an enormous carving knife as Steve
lifts the cover off the turkey: there, surrounded by roasted
vegetables, is the head of the Young Boy, his eyes closed,
waxy in death. Addie hesitates.)*

GEMMA: Dark meat for me, please.
JOAN: Me, too.
HAT: I'll take an ear to start, I'm not all that hungry.
TUCKER: What's wrong, old girl? You okay?
HAT: Mom?
ADDIE: I'm fine, I'm fine, I was just thinking . . . all the good
    times we've had.
TUCKER: Here . . .

*(He reaches around Addie, helping her guide the knife
down to the boy's head.)*

ADDIE: Thank you.

(As the knife meets the boy's neck, his eyes fly open.)

YOUNG BOY: Ow!

(Addie recoils.)

TUCKER: It's all right, it's not gonna bite you.
ADDIE: I know.
YOUNG BOY: Go ahead. You might as well.

(None of the others react to the Young Boy.)

ADDIE: What . . . what do you mean?
YOUNG BOY: Anyone who would rhyme "chaos" with "Laos."
ADDIE: What?
YOUNG BOY: Or allow the meter to fall apart, even *think* that
    was something worth doing . . .
ADDIE: Well . . .
YOUNG BOY: "A clock upon the wall of fate"! Kill me, please,
    I want to die.
ADDIE: No, you . . .
YOUNG BOY: YES!
ADDIE: I . . .
YOUNG BOY: I WANT TO! I WANT IT!

*(The Young Boy's hands leap up through the roasted veg-
etables and seize the knife handle, driving the blade deep
into his own neck: copious blood spurts up, splattering
Addie, who screams. Everyone runs off as Addie slams the
cover back on the turkey and falls back onto the sofa, covering herself with the blanket, moaning.*

*Lights change to reveal the room in morning light, Addie
hopelessly tangled in the blanket. She wakes, holds her
head. The turkey platter and all the other plates of food
remain where they were. Steve descends the stairs.)*

ADDIE: Good morning. Want . . . ? Help yourself, Steven,
    anything.
STEVE: Would you like some juice?
ADDIE: Yes, fine. Thanks. Please, I mean. *(She turns, knocking
    over a wine bottle or wineglass—or both)* Oh . . . oh.

(Steve pours two glasses of juice and brings them into the living room.)

STEVE: Here you go.

ADDIE: Thank you. *(The glass slips from Addie's fingers, spilling its entire contents)*

STEVE: I'll get it, just relax. It's okay. I don't mind. *(He runs into the kitchen for paper towels and returns to clean up the spill during:)* I hate when the first thing that happens in the day is bad, that happens all the time. Then you've gotta like either go back to sleep or just, you know, give up.

ADDIE *(Eyeing the platter)*: Oh. What happened to the turkey?

(During Steve's following speech, Addie reaches for the lid of the turkey platter, hesitates, then lifts it: there, as before, is the head of the Young Boy, eyes and mouth now wide open. Addie replaces the lid.)

STEVE: Well, um . . . I came back and you were asleep, so I took it out and let it cool, and you were still asleep, and I tried to wake Joan, and she didn't come out, so I thought, Well, cold turkey is good, too, and I was full from the pie, so I went for a walk, and you were still asleep, and so . . .

ADDIE: Where was Hat in all this? Gemma's?

STEVE: He, maybe he came back when I was out. So I went to bed and spent the night with Tucker. *(He indicates the book of poems)* They're really good, I think. I mean . . . Well . . . I enjoyed them. A lot.

ADDIE: Some Thanksgiving.

STEVE: Oh, no, it was so much better than my family would have been . . . Really, I mean that. My mother would've found something to say to make me and my sister feel really bad, something we didn't do right, something we weren't born with, some trait, like . . . I don't know . . . height. *(He offers Addie a sip of his orange juice)*

ADDIE: Thank you.

STEVE: Got it? She's got this boyfriend now who's about two weeks older than I am practically. I don't know, he says he's thirty-six, I think he's probably . . . twenty-three. Really. Or . . . twenty-nine at the very oldest. But my sister thinks she doesn't want us around to remind him how old she actually is.

ADDIE: Your sister's probably right.

STEVE: So this is the best Thanksgiving I've had in . . . ever, basically.

ADDIE: Well, that's somewhat . . . tragic in my view.

STEVE: Yeah. You said it.

ADDIE: I have . . . got to put some kind of order into my life. Six months ago I thought I was close to finishing a book. Then my son came to live at home with his then-wife.

STEVE: Oh, he was married, too?

(A beat; Addie can make no sense of this remark and decides she doesn't have to.)

ADDIE: I'm sorry, I was yawning.

STEVE: You know . . . I used to drink all through junior high. It really messes up your self-esteem. I know that sounds funny. It does. You gotta like . . . You can't let that: "Here I am at the bottom of a well, want to drink some pond scum?" feeling tell you what you're really worth. You can't.

ADDIE: You're right.

STEVE: 'Cause . . . And glue is worse. In case you're wondering.

(The Young Boy reappears near Addie—from behind or within the sofa.)

YOUNG BOY: Okay, that's it, get him out of here. Please? Please, Mom?

STEVE: But . . .

YOUNG BOY: Tell him the room is rented as of tonight.

STEVE: The thing? . . . that got me to stop drinking? This . . . Okay, you'll probably say this is — . . .

YOUNG BOY: Stupid, right, so don't bother—

STEVE: . . . was the realization that . . . in all of eternity . . . all the billions of centuries before now and all the billions yet to come . . . I mean, either like before we were born or after we die . . .

YOUNG BOY: "Like, yeah, like . . ."

STEVE: I mean, all the times it could be right now . . . like the Stone Age or the future, way way in the future when you and I are so dead it isn't funny . . .

(The Young Boy perches on the back of the sofa, pretending to strangle himself.)

But *in fact* . . . the incredible thing is that in all of that vast expanse of time it *could be*—

YOUNG BOY: STOP HIM!!!!

STEVE: . . . It isn't! It's just exactly now at this one particular . . . instant when we're alive . . . Isn't that . . . ? And I didn't want to . . . It's so *Buddhist,* right?, I didn't want to waste it . . .

YOUNG BOY: Aaaaaaa!

(Without looking at him, Addie shoves the Young Boy off the back of the sofa. Then, disappearing from view:)

Mom!

ADDIE: You're absolutely right, Steven, we shouldn't waste it! I'm glad to hear someone put it so bluntly. Help me clean up in here. I'm quitting drinking as of today.

STEVE: Well, that's the other thing. You shouldn't make promises you can't keep: you should just like . . .

ADDIE: One day at a time.

STEVE: That's right. So if you fail, it's only that day, it isn't your whole life.

ADDIE: Good point.

(Tucker appears out of nowhere, directly in Addie's path.)

TUCKER: God grant me the grace to know the difference between a rat's ass and his so-called brain!

(Addie changes direction; the Young Boy reappears, also in her way.)

YOUNG BOY: Go, Dad!

ADDIE: We'll start by getting some fresh air in here, what do you say? *(She walks to the front door and opens it. To Tucker and the Young Boy)* Out. The two of you. Out. Now.

YOUNG BOY: It's cold.

ADDIE: Good. That's the way I like it. "Go, dad! Go, son!"

TUCKER: Never stay where you're not welcome.

(Through the following, Tucker and the Young Boy trudge out; Addie closes the door. She and Steve begin carrying the platters of uneaten food into the kitchen and begin to wrap up the food and scrape the plates.)

ADDIE: The good thing about not having eaten is there aren't too many dishes to clean up.

STEVE: That's true. You know what I mean, though? And it's how I got through last semester.

ADDIE: What do you mean?

STEVE: Whenever I had to do homework, you know, which was every night—

ADDIE: Right.

STEVE: I didn't say, "Well, I'm doing it now, that means I'll *always* do it," I just said, "Well, tonight I have the choice of doing my homework or not, but I could be a total fuck-up tomorrow," so I was reserving for myself the right to go back to letting my mother down and that was all I needed to get it done, more or less.

ADDIE: That's . . . astonishing, Steve.

STEVE: I know. I even surprised myself, but it worked so . . .

ADDIE: Why argue with success?

STEVE: Exactly.

ADDIE: I'll wash and you dry. All right?
STEVE: Sure.

(Addie steps on a pedal to lift the lid on the trash container, and the Young Boy pops up from within; Addie makes a concerted effort to ignore him.)

YOUNG BOY: You always did all the work; all my homework, all my yard work, all the dishes; I never had to struggle at anything: I had to be so brilliant, I couldn't even be ordinary.
ADDIE *(To Steve)*: Here. *(She hands Steve the garbage)*
STEVE: Thanks.
YOUNG BOY: It was too much of a threat to your self-image for me to have to work, because that would mean I wasn't a total genius, which I wasn't, no matter how much you wanted me to be one, so what did you get in the end?
ADDIE *(To Steve)*: That's fine.
YOUNG BOY: A divorced son living at home with his mother and his ex-wife at the age of thirty, selling slag.
ADDIE *(To Steve)*: I actually like to wash dishes: it's soothing, you know? *(To the Young Boy, without skipping a beat)* Marianne Moore lived with her mother into her seventies, and she published some perfectly decent poems.
YOUNG BOY: Oh, great, that's what I want to be, some sexless seventy-year-old Yankee poet writing about zoo animals, posing for the cover of *Life* magazine with Mom, both of us in three-cornered hats—

(Tucker appears from inside a cabinet. He has two three-cornered hats, each with gray wigs attached; he places one on Addie and the other on the Young Boy.)

Terrific, there's something to aspire to.

(The Young Boy turns Addie toward an invisible photographer as a flashbulb goes off in her face. Throughout the fol-

*lowing, Tucker and the Young Boy behave as forces of anar-
chy, making every possible form of mischief to distract and
frustrate Addie.)*

ADDIE: Wallace Stevens sold insurance and he didn't do badly.
   Van Gogh didn't start to paint until he was thirty.
YOUNG BOY: Now there's a good role model.
TUCKER: Mmmm.

*(The Young Boy saws off his ear with a bread knife and
hands it to Addie; she drops it into the garbage disposal and
flips the switch, turning it on very briefly, during which
time Tucker applies Van Gogh's famous bandage to the Young
Boy's ear, and the Young Boy produces a pipe and poses for
another flash.)*

ADDIE: Amy Clampitt didn't publish until she was sixty.
TUCKER: Probably waiting for her mother to die.
ADDIE *(To Steve)*: One of the things I think I appreciate about
   you most, Steven, is your seeming lack of irony. You
   don't take that as an insult, do you?
STEVE: Irony?
TUCKER: Ironing?
YOUNG BOY: Did she say ironing?
TUCKER: HO!

*(Tucker produces a hot iron and tosses it to the Young Boy;
they begin juggling kitchen items.)*

ADDIE: You know: meaning something other than the literal
   words you're speaking, implying through a kind of
   humorous, well, it's a lot like sarcasm. Reversing the
   meaning of what you say.
STEVE: Okay.
ADDIE: Twisting it.
TUCKER: Rhetorically.
YOUNG BOY: Like hyperbole!
TUCKER: Litotes!

YOUNG BOY: Gesundheit!

STEVE *(Is he being mocked?)*: Well . . . thanks.

ADDIE: You're welcome. No, I'm serious. It's one of your most endearing qualities. I was genuinely praising you.

TUCKER: Right.

YOUNG BOY: Right.

ADDIE: I was, I wasn't being ironic myself.

YOUNG BOY: Even he doesn't believe you.

ADDIE: I wasn't!

STEVE: Okay.

(Tucker and the Young Boy manage to pass Addie something pointed and dangerous or unwieldy; whatever it is, it is unexpected and she drops it at her feet with a loud thud. Steve stops, staring at Addie, then down at whatever has fallen. Addie picks it up and sets it on the counter.)

ADDIE: Excuse me a moment, Steven, won't you?

(She turns and walks into the living room in an effort to regain her composure. Tucker and the Young Boy follow her in; Joan appears in her nightgown, descending the stairs.)

JOAN: Hi.

ADDIE: Good morning, Joan.

TUCKER AND YOUNG BOY: Morning!

JOAN: Good morning.

ADDIE: How'd you sleep?

TUCKER AND YOUNG BOY: Not bad, you?

JOAN *(Overlapping slightly)*: Oh . . . not so good. How's your shin?

ADDIE: Oh, I'd forgotten, honestly.

TUCKER: Liar!

JOAN: I'm sorry.

ADDIE: Don't be.

YOUNG BOY: You broke up my marriage, too, 'case you didn't realize it.

JOAN: Where's Hat?

TUCKER: Fucking Gemma.

JOAN: What time'd he get back?

YOUNG BOY: Never.

ADDIE: He . . .

(Without warning, Addie pulls the Civil War sword off the wall and skewers Tucker straight through the heart; he moans, staggering. She opens the cellar door in time for him to stumble in. At the last second she yanks the sword out of him, then slams the door shut as he is heard falling noisily down the length of stairs.)

YOUNG BOY *(Keeping his distance)*: I didn't say anything!

ADDIE *(Indicating the sword to Joan)*: I keep meaning to get this appraised . . . Steve came back first.

(Joan gives a little, obligatory nod. Addie wipes the sword down and returns it to the wall; Joan starts toward the kitchen.)

Joan? . . . Of course I like you, I've always liked you. You're refreshing and spontaneous, and I'm mad as hell you're hurting my boy.

JOAN: I know.

ADDIE: I realize there are times when I have probably made you feel as if I didn't approve of you without even having to say a word . . . and I apologize.

JOAN: Oh. Well . . .

ADDIE: You're welcome. I mean . . .

JOAN: Thank you.

ADDIE: I knew you were going to say it.

JOAN: I know.

ADDIE: But . . . I don't think you should stay here. Do you? I think this has been a mistake.

JOAN: . . . Okay.

ADDIE: All right? *(Short pause)* You understand, don't you?

JOAN: Of course. *(Small pause)* You know . . . I spent so much time worrying about whether or not you approved of me, I never even stopped to think how I felt about you.

ADDIE: Oh dear. Now you're going to tell me, aren't you?

JOAN: Not if you don't want me to.

ADDIE: No, go ahead. I make you feel . . . angry. Insecure. Frustrated.

JOAN: Sad.

ADDIE: Sad?

JOAN: I used to think, Why is she using all those puns all the time? In your articles, your reviews.

(A silent "Ah" from Addie.)

You'll take a word from the person's title or from their last name and use it to mean something else—

ADDIE: I know what a pun is—I'm sorry.

JOAN: I know I should be able to give you an example, I know I'm unconscious, I've read everything you've written about consciousness, and I agree, completely, I do: people should see and notice and remember everything, appreciate . . . I assumed you did it, made all those puns, because you thought it amused your readers, but . . . well, I can't imagine anyone liking it; it seems cruel. You're better than that. It seems . . . smartass. Like you're frightened.

(Pause.)

YOUNG BOY: I feel sad for you, too, Mom. Sad—well, more like pity, really.

(Addie stands; the Young Boy backs away.)

JOAN: Sorry.

ADDIE: No, I have to pee, I can't hold it anymore, but I appreciate your candor, Joan, I do . . . I'm sure on some level you're—

(Addie opens the bathroom door. Tucker is standing in there; she pulls him out.)

TUCKER *(Heads for the front door)*: Well, I'm off to fix Mrs. Bieler's radio!
ADDIE *(Disappearing into bathroom)*: Right.
TUCKER: Sun's out! *(He exits)*

(The Young Boy reaches the front door just in time for it to slam shut in his face, reverberating loudly, as before.)

YOUNG BOY: Dad?

(The Young Boy stands, looking out. Joan moves into the kitchen.)

JOAN: Good morning.
STEVE: Hey. I knocked on your door when the turkey was done, but . . .
JOAN: I was paralyzed.
STEVE: We were missing you. I was anyway.
JOAN: Oh. Well, can I offer you a ride somewhere today, Steve?
STEVE: Maybe. Where are you going?
JOAN: I don't really know. I have some friends I guess I can call.
STEVE: Okay. Yeah. Maybe I'll go with you.
JOAN: All right. You want coffee?

(Steve nods. Joan starts to make coffee. He comes up behind her, pushes the hair off her neck and kisses her there.)

What? No, no. It's not you . . . You're very nice, I'm much older than you are, and I'm on the rebound.
STEVE: The guy who used to live here?
JOAN: Right.
STEVE: You were married to.

JOAN: That's right.

STEVE: Hat's dad.

JOAN: No! Hat's dad?

STEVE: Wasn't he the poet? Wasn't —?

JOAN: Hat's a poet, too, they're both poets.

STEVE: Oh.

JOAN: Hat is the other guy; we were married, up until and including this past week, I'm sorry.

STEVE: Ohhhh.

JOAN: I was toying with you yesterday in a stupid and mean way when I said all that stuff.

STEVE: I'm not always too . . .

JOAN: Yes, you are, you're perfectly . . . whatever . . . you—and I'm flattered about just now, I am, honest. I just . . .

STEVE: I think you're real attractive.

JOAN: Well, that's the outside. But thanks. You're attractive on the outside, too. Probably on the in.

STEVE: Do I have time to take a shower?

JOAN: Sure. I'm in no hurry to start my life all over with nowhere to live, no job.

STEVE: They're always hiring at the Food Lion.

JOAN: You're . . . That's very sweet. Maybe. We'll see.

(Their eyes connect.)

STEVE: *Come on.*

(He and Joan kiss. Addie comes out of the bathroom, followed by Tucker.)

TUCKER: Remember the time you told me I wasn't taking enough risks in my work?

(Addie starts down the stairs only to be met by:)

YOUNG BOY: How do you think it felt to be the only child of socialist atheists in Republican P.A.?

(Addie wheels around and goes back up the stairs, followed by both of them.)

TUCKER: Take a look at the risks Robert Lowell is taking!

YOUNG BOY: My biggest fantasy was I'd be on my deathbed and you and Dad would be there, and with my last, weakest breath I would say, "I believe in God!" and I would die!

ADDIE *(From off)*: Go to hell and see how you like it!

(Addie, Tucker and the Young Boy exit above. Joan disengages from the kiss.)

JOAN: That's enough now.

STEVE *(Looking down)*: Look what you did to me.

JOAN: Well, a breeze or even some small animal jumping up and down in your lap can accomplish the same thing, so I won't take it as too much of a . . . Go take your shower . . . before . . .

(She moves away from him, but Steve follows her to the far corner of the kitchen.)

All right, that's, that's—

(She pats him as he tries to kiss her again; at the same moment, Hat comes in the back door; he is wearing the same clothes from the night before. Joan steps self-consciously away from Steve, who guiltily turns to face Hat.)

Good morning!

STEVE: Hey.

HAT: Hey!

(Steve turns and exits up the stairs.)

JOAN: We didn't do anything.

HAT: Oh?

JOAN: You're up early.

HAT: How was the turkey, anyway?

JOAN: You didn't have any?

HAT: Nope.

JOAN: Me either. I think she must have been covering for you. Your mom. She wanted me to think you came home last night. Did you sleep with her?

HAT: It's against the law to sleep with your mom, you know that.

JOAN: Did you?

HAT: As a matter of fact I did, yes. It was nice. She was nice, it felt good.

JOAN: Well, good.

HAT: Which is of course the idea. I've . . . I realize . . . missed being . . .

JOAN: Adored.

HAT: Okay. I'll go along with that.

JOAN: Me, too.

HAT: Uhn-un, we're not going to mythologize what took place here as your having been neglected in any way.

JOAN: I meant I'd go along with your feeling that.

HAT: Oh. Right.

(Small pause.)

JOAN: Can I ask you, though? I mean . . . What did we believe in? You and me. You know?

HAT: No.

JOAN: What did we think was actually worth passing on to our kids if we had had them?

HAT: Oh, I see, now we're gonna have them in retrospect so you can make me guilty for fucking them up in your imagination?

JOAN: Sure . . . But do you not even hear that? How do you ever expect, I mean, to create anything with that voice taking a crap all over it before it even has a chance to get up and walk around, try out its new little legs for itself. You know—?

HAT *(Overlapping slightly)*: Art. Yes, okay, I believe in art. Thank you. Nothing else in the world, not even sex, love, justice . . . provides the same permanent solace. What do you believe in then that's so fucking . . . ?

JOAN *(Overlapping)*: Honest? Honestly?

HAT: No, try a lie first and work your way up. Is that the voice? All right, I concede.

JOAN: I believe in getting a job and living life without undue stress, and being considerate and kind to yourself and your family and not trying to delve into it all, and not making everybody miserable so you and/or they can all meet some . . . *standard* that is totally unattainable except by a few godlike creatures once every couple of centuries who were probably all mean to their friends and family anyway.

HAT: You believe in "nice."

JOAN: No, I — . . . What—? *Yes*, what's wrong with nice, Hat?

HAT: Nothing. Except if—there—

JOAN *(Overlapping)*: If you, I'll tell you something, if you went down in history as unquestionably the greatest poet who ever lived, better than Shakespeare and Dante and all those other yahoos, I would still say, "Was he nice? Was he kind?" And if the answer is no, I'd say, "So? So *what?*" "Let me compare thee to a summer's day." Fuck that, be nice to people, we're all gonna be dead soon enough, god!

HAT: You're right. Can't we try? Just . . . ? Please stay, please. *(Small pause)* That was the wrong thing to say, wasn't it?

JOAN *(Starting up the stairs)*: It's like there's an invisible army of breathers in here, I'm suffocating. I've gotta go, I'm sorry.

HAT: You had to be saving that up; nobody pulls a line like that out of their butt.

JOAN *(Not stopping)*: Right. As always.

(Addie appears on the landing, dressed.)

HAT: Just an observation.

(Joan passes Addie, exiting above. Addie is followed down the stairs by the Young Boy, Tucker and Steve, all of whom trail after her down to the landing; Steve disappears into the bathroom; the others follow Addie into the living room.)

ADDIE: G'morning.

(Hat does not respond.)

Want some turkey?

TUCKER: Is that what you would want someone to say to you?

YOUNG BOY: Why do people always offer you food when they sense grief?

TUCKER: Good question. Here's a riddle: why is grief like an ocean?

(Addie sits by Hat.)

YOUNG BOY: Why is grief like an ocean?

ADDIE: Sweetheart.

YOUNG BOY: . . . like an ocean . . .

ADDIE: I know . . . *(Short pause)* I want . . . to strike some sort of . . . We're on, lately, the wrong footing, the two of us, and I feel . . .

YOUNG BOY: Sorrow, despair . . .

ADDIE: . . . as frustrated as I'm sure you do . . . too . . .

TUCKER: Give up?

YOUNG BOY: Wait.

ADDIE: Do you think living here, all of us, has been a good idea? Has been good for us both, for our —?

HAT: You're throwing me out?

ADDIE: No.

HAT: What are you saying?

ADDIE: I'm . . .

HAT *(Overlapping)*: You're throwing me out.

ADDIE: You're—no—

HAT *(Continuous, overlapping)*: My wife is leaving me, my poetry sucks, according to you—

ADDIE: Your poetry does not suck.

HAT *(Continuous, overlapping)*: —and you're evicting me?

ADDIE: I'm not—

HAT *(Continuous; standing, moving up the stairs)*: Gemma's invited me to move in and I'm taking her up on it, so, but thanks for the vote of confidence! Ma—!

ADDIE: You're completely misunderstanding—

HAT *(Ascending, overlapping)*: No, I'm not. *(He disappears upstairs)*

ADDIE: I am not. Wait!—

TUCKER *(Overlapping)*: Time's up!

YOUNG BOY: Wait, I said—

TUCKER: Grief is like an ocean because it seems infinite when you're riding in the middle of it, but you're—

YOUNG BOY: Oh, right.

TUCKER: —sure to reach the shore someday if you—

YOUNG BOY AND TUCKER: —keep riding the waves.

YOUNG BOY: Right.

ADDIE *(With every ounce of patience she has left)*: Tucker? Hat?

(They look at her.)

I need you both . . . *(She moves to the back of the sofa)* Would you . . . *(She gestures for them to come closer)* Come in, come in close.

(She draws them near to her, as if she is about to say something in earnest; suddenly with all her strength she bangs their heads together, and they recoil in pain.)

TUCKER: OW!

YOUNG BOY: OH!

(Addie walks into the kitchen. Tucker and the Young Boy hold their heads.)

JOAN *(From above, offstage)*: I'm almost finished.

HAT *(From above, offstage)*: Take your time. I'll be out of your way in two secs.

(The sounds of dresser drawers being opened, closed; closet doors slammed, suitcases opened.)

That's mine, sorry.

JOAN *(From off)*: No, it's not.

HAT *(From off)*: You want it? You can keep it.

JOAN *(From off)*: I . . . No, I thought it was mine.

HAT *(From off)*: It is now. See? Isn't that easy?

JOAN *(From off)*: Steve? If you're gonna come with me . . .

STEVE *(From off)*: Be right there!

(Joan appears on the landing, dressed, and with two hastily packed suitcases, which she lugs down the stairs. Tucker and the Young Boy watch.)

JOAN: I'm gonna drop Steve over at the Food Lion, see if they still have his clothes. Then, I don't know, I'll call you when I know where I'm staying.

ADDIE: I didn't mean you had to leave this minute.

JOAN: No, this is much better. It is. Really.

ADDIE: Well . . . good luck.

JOAN: Thank you. I appreciate it.

(Joan kisses Addie. At the same time, Hat appears on the landing, with a suitcase and a shopping bag filled with hastily packed clothes and other items. Steve emerges from the bathroom at this instant; he, too, is dressed.)

HAT: Oh, Steve, do me a favor, would you? Stand right here for a second. Right over . . .

(Hat puts down his luggage and positions Steve at the very edge of the top step.)

Good. Right there. Great.

STEVE: Well . . .

HAT: Perfect. Now close your eyes, would you? Go ahead, I won't hurt you . . . Promise. I swear.

(Steve reluctantly shuts his eyes, peeking out through slits.)

No, keep 'em tight. Keep . . . Good . . . A few more seconds. *(Pause)* Great. That was perfect, thanks a lot.

STEVE: I don't get it.

HAT *(Carrying the luggage downstairs)*: Good. Now you know how I feel all the time. Mom, you know where all my underwear and socks are?

JOAN: Bye, Hat.

HAT: Bye. *(Without pausing)* Do you? Mom?

ADDIE: I'm sure they're in the drier if they're not upstairs.

(Steve descends into the living room. Hat starts selecting books from the shelves and packing them in one of his bags.)

Steve, I'm sorry I abandoned you in the middle of our clean-up duty.

STEVE: Oh, that's okay—

ADDIE: Your next meal I hope we get to enjoy when it comes out of the oven.

STEVE: Me, too. You, too. I mean . . .

ADDIE: And your mother will get over it, I promise. If you wear clothes, she'll think about it a lot less.

STEVE: Oh—

ADDIE: Your being younger. Didn't you say something about . . . ?

STEVE: Right. Right.

(Steve starts for the door, then returns to Addie for a full-fledged hug.)

JOAN: I'll call when I know where I'm going to be.

(Hat stops packing books for:)

HAT: Okay, bye, take it easy.
JOAN: You, too.

(Joan and Hat hug, keeping their groins far apart. Steve is almost out the front door.)

HAT *(With great, false cheer)*: Bye, Steve!
STEVE: Bye. *(He holds the door open for Joan)*
ADDIE: Bye now.
TUCKER: Bye!
YOUNG BOY: Bye!

(Joan's bag gets caught on the door frame.)

HAT *(Moves to help with the door)*: Here—
JOAN: That's okay.

(Steve and Joan exit. The door slams in Hat's face; the sound reverberates loudly, as before.)

(From outside) Whoops, bye.

(Hat stands at the door, looking out, as Steve and Joan disappear. Sound of the car starting up, driving away. Addie, Tucker and the Young Boy all look at Hat.)

YOUNG BOY: Great work, Mom, really.

(The Young Boy walks into the kitchen. Addie turns, slowly following him in.)

ADDIE *(Evenly)*: You think I'll live forever, but I won't, and you only get one mother, you'll see. You'll see. You think the things you say won't come back to haunt you. But they will. Every single second of your life you tried to make me suffer, after I'm gone, you'll see:

you'll play it all back and regret it, every single moment of it, every single moment! *(Covers her face)* Everything . . . everything . . .

(Addie rushes into the cellar. The Young Boy follows her, calling down.)

YOUNG BOY: Mom? . . .
ADDIE *(From off)*: Go away!

(The Young Boy disappears after her. Hat now turns and sees Tucker for the first time.)

HAT: Oh god . . . Don't say anything, please: no palliatives, leave me no homilies, no helpful aphorisms . . . thanks. *(He resumes combing through the shelves for books, which he packs into his bags)* The preferred legacy by far would have been talent. That and the unshakable belief in that, so . . . All right, let me just . . . one question, okay?
TUCKER: Your ball game.
HAT: Why wouldn't she want me to succeed? You ever figure that out?
TUCKER: Who says she doesn't? Maybe she wants it too much.
HAT: Uh-huh.
TUCKER: Maybe her need is too great.
HAT: Thanks a lot. Back to oblivion for you. *(He makes the loud sound of a buzzer on a game show: "Wrong answer!")*
TUCKER: Maybe if she knew how poems were made, and how they grew . . .
HAT: Right.
TUCKER: . . . and how one must fall flat on one's face and fail and fail again and keep failing until a door opens in the rock-face, she wouldn't be living her life for masterpieces, but for failures. As every sports fan will tell ya: a season is made up of losses and more losses.
HAT: Where are you getting these sports images? Look, it would be gratifying to have this talk; it would . . . and

maybe we will. Maybe the dead will come back, maybe . . . beauty and truth will triumph over commerce, maybe I won't blow my brains out the way I'm pretty sure you must've. How else could you have kept away from her all this time?

TUCKER: How indeed?

(Pause.)

HAT: I have a diatribe brewing, always, and I could expel it all in my sleep even, a thousand of them probably, but each and every word of each and every one sounds . . . exactly . . .

TUCKER: Like her.

HAT: I know I'm being an asshole; it's like watching an accident.

TUCKER: Uh-huh.

HAT: I know everything I'm going to say and do before I do it, I know how absurd it is, I can see the crash, feel the ludicrosity of my actions, is there such a word?

TUCKER: Say there is.

HAT: What a brat I am about to be . . . And I'm powerless to stop the force . . . I stand back . . . "Don't!" Flying glass . . . limbs . . . Where are you? I won't tell.

(Hat and Tucker stare at each other. Gemma appears at the back door, knocks before letting herself in.)

No?

GEMMA: Hello? May I . . . ? Morning. You snuck out.

HAT: Well, I'm sneaking right back. If that's all right.

GEMMA: You're . . . Oh.

HAT: Is that still okay? . . . Last night was nice, it really was. It was more than nice. It felt . . . it felt very, very good. You're . . . well, you're a wonderful lover.

GEMMA: Oh, go on. Say more.

HAT: I'm . . . guess I'm . . . I think I'm a little discombobulated just this second . . .

(Gemma nods. Addie and the Young Boy come up from the cellar with the laundry hamper, filled with folded socks and underwear.)

GEMMA: It's . . .
HAT: What?

(Addie and the Young Boy hold stock-still.)

GEMMA: I thought about Hammy the whole time we were making love.
HAT: Oh. I understand. Of course you did.
GEMMA: And . . . thinking about him was . . . not what I wanted to be doing.
HAT: No. I un—
GEMMA: And . . . I would want to be with you if I am going to be with you.

(Pause. Hat nods. Addie and the Young Boy ease their way back into the stairwell.)

HAT: Well, maybe . . . maybe we can date.
GEMMA: Yes. In a little while. I want to.
HAT: Me, too. Yes. I mean, unless it's . . .
GEMMA: No. I mean, we'll see. *(Short pause)* Thank you. *(Pause)* I wanted to tell Joan I was sorry for last night.
HAT: She's gone. With the Food Lion himself.
GEMMA: What a good and attractive man you are. I'm very . . . excited that you—
HAT: That's . . . Good, good, me too.
GEMMA: I am.
HAT: I am, too. No, I am. Oh, these fucking . . . *(Indicates his bags)* Why won't they . . . evaporate?

(Gemma takes the bags from him and sets them down gently, deliberately.)

GEMMA: I don't always . . . organize or plan things right.
HAT: It's okay.

' want . . . We're gonna work out. But . . . I need
...ne. That's all.

(She kisses him.)

You want to come over for lunch?
HAT: Sure. Maybe.
GEMMA: The girls . . . I think the girls should get used to you.
HAT: We'll see . . .
GEMMA: The idea. Stop being a neighbor, be more of a
boyfriend.

(Impulsively, she kisses him again, this time passionately.)

Call me.

*(Short pause. She leaves. Hat looks at the suitcase and
shopping bags. Tucker helps him return his books to the
shelves. Addie and the Young Boy come up from the cellar
once more.)*

ADDIE: Your socks and underwear are here, but you misun-
derstood what I was saying, I wasn't asking—
HAT *(His father's chapbook in hand)*: Are these any good really?
Do you think?
ADDIE: I thought they were. I wanted them to be. Your
poems do not suck.
HAT: No idea why he left?
ADDIE: Oh, I haven't thought about it in years.

*(Tucker stands at the bookshelves; Addie momentarily
catches his eye.)*

Me, primarily. But then . . . your father was probably
gay, sweetie.
HAT: He was?
ADDIE: And he left me, he didn't leave you.
HAT: Same difference. But I mean, were there clues? That he
was?

ADDIE: No, not really. There were clues that he wasn't serious, or as serious about his work as I thought he should be . . . He liked to drink, for one thing. I like to drink, too, but not before eleven.

HAT: Oh, wow.

ADDIE: What time is it now? . . . He was a wonderful, fun, if callow soul.

HAT: Did you feel exploited by him?

ADDIE: You mean sexually? Oh, financially. No, not at all. I had the money, I could help. Our politics were such a tangle of guilt and—crap and good intentions, anyway.

HAT: But . . .

ADDIE: He was good in bed. As they go.

HAT: Then why did you think he was gay?

ADDIE: Oh, it's a theory and I like it, I find it useful, whatever its basis in fact. Bisexual. He was such an "art boy," you know. Hard to tell.

HAT: "Art boy"?

ADDIE: I heard one of my students say that the other day.

HAT: Joan isn't gay. I don't think. She used to love . . . oh, who knows what she loved, she said she loved my poems, too, so . . . *(Pause)* Would you read the rest of them some time?

(Addie shakes her head no.)

You won't? Why? Are you—?

ADDIE: I think . . . any artist worth their salt should write things, paint things, that their mother would despise, don't you?

HAT: Of course. But are you saying you did? Despise them?

ADDIE *(Overlapping slightly)*: No. No! But . . . just exactly that . . . Sometimes I think the best thing that can happen to any of us is the worst thing we can imagine. And vice versa. *(Short pause)* Careful what you wish for . . . What if I loved them? That would be worse, wouldn't it?

HAT: Why?

ADDIE: I'd have to love all of them from here on out: this way you're free.

HAT: Right. *(Pause)* Right. No, you're right. You are.

(Addie nods. Pause.)

ADDIE: My idea of heaven . . . not that you asked . . . is the attainment of aesthetic bliss. I've said it before.

(Hat nods.)

Well, I'll say it again, indulge me.

HAT: Okay.

ADDIE: If I were a writer, I think I'd be my ideal—the perfect reader . . . Every book, every story, poem seems to me to have been written expressly for me, and me alone: it arrives intact—

HAT: Mm-hm.

ADDIE: . . . perfectly preserved from whatever time and place, wrapped in some kind of . . . metaphysical Saran Wrap: direct from Laurence Sterne or Marvell, Poe. Marilyn Hacker. But . . . I wouldn't know how to help you get there any more than I would know— . . . And maybe you're already there. There are plenty of good writers I simply don't get.

HAT: You're condescending to me.

ADDIE: I'm not.

HAT: It's all right, but . . .

ADDIE: Oh . . . maybe I am. *(She sticks her tongue out at him)* So there.

HAT: Thank you.

ADDIE: If Eudora Welty asked me how to help with "A Curtain of Green," I think my blood would freeze . . . I'd die.

HAT *(Almost silent)*: Uh-huh.

ADDIE: I'm an appreciator: that's my talent. I want to cheer you on . . . but I can't get you there, much as I might wish I could. I'm terrible at it. If anything sucks it's my ability to do that.

TUCKER: *Now* you tell us.
ADDIE *(To Tucker)*: Yes.
YOUNG BOY: Well?
HAT: So?
TUCKER: Well, all right, I was— . . . Fine.

(Pause.)

HAT: Have you ever thought . . . I'm sure you have.
ADDIE: What?
HAT: There are really only two jobs in the whole world that are self-appointed? You don't need any qualification whatsoever.
ADDIE: Artist and critic.
HAT: Right. Well, parent, too, I guess.

(Addie nods. A beat.)

ADDIE: True.
HAT: Now that I think . . .
ADDIE: Terrorists.
HAT: Right. There are a lot, I guess. All related. *(Pause. He picks up a book, opens it)* Who was it . . . said, "True intimacy is the ability to sit in silence and read with someone"?
ADDIE: Lots of people . . . But that isn't the most intimate . . .
HAT: It's not?

(Addie stands.)

ADDIE: And it isn't what people think, either.

(Hat watches as Addie pulls a chair up to her desk, pulls out her notes and the manuscript for her book, and begins organizing the pages. Hat sits for another moment, then reaches into his suitcase and pulls out a sheaf of his poems. He looks through them. Hat moves to the far end of the room and sits in a window seat. Addie begins to type, stops.)

Will this bother you?

(Hat shakes his head no. He looks again at his poems, finds a pencil, looks for a legal pad. Tucker locates it, gives it to him. Hat begins to scribble; the Young Boy drifts to Addie's side. She smiles, keeps working. Tucker stands beside Hat, looking directly over his shoulder.)

TUCKER: No reason you can't rhyme "Laos" with "chaos." After all: "God is great, God is good, and we thank him for our food!" *(He pronounces "food" as "fud" to rhyme with "good")*

(Hat keeps working.)

The meter falling apart here is one of the best things about the poem. What doesn't work is the transition: when you think something's wrong, look back; the problem's usually in the setup. The wrong expectations. See?

(Addie is typing. Hat is working on his poem. Tucker reads over Hat's shoulder.)

Good. Very good.

(The Young Boy points to the page in Addie's typewriter.)

YOUNG BOY: Two "m"s in "committed."
ADDIE: Thank you.

(Addie and Hat continue working, the Young Boy and Tucker looking on. Lights fade.)

END OF PLAY

THREE POSTCARDS

A MUSICAL PLAY

WITH MUSIC AND LYRICS BY CRAIG CARNELIA

For Norman René

Three Postcards was originally produced at South Coast Repertory (David Emmes, Producing Artistic Director; Martin Benson, Artistic Director) in Costa Mesa, California, on January 6, 1987. It was directed by Norman René; the set design was by Loy Arcenas, the costume design was by Walker Hicklin, the lighting design was by Debra J. Kletter, the sound design was by Bruce D. Cameron, the choreography was by Linda Kostalik-Boussom, the dramaturg was John Glore and the stage manager was Julie Haber. The cast was as follows:

BILL	Craig Carnelia
WALTER	Brad O'Hare
BIG JANE	Jane Galloway
LITTLE JANE	Maureen Silliman
K.C.	Karen Trott

Three Postcards opened at Playwrights Horizons (André Bishop, Artistic Director; Paul S. Daniels, Executive Director; Ira Weitzman, Musical Theatre Program Director) in New York City, on May 14, 1987. It was directed by Norman René; the set design was by Loy Arcenas, the costume design was by Walker Hicklin, the lighting design was by Debra J. Kletter, the sound design was by Bruce D. Cameron, the choreography was by Linda Kostalik-Boussom and the stage manager was M. A. Howard. The cast was as follows:

BILL	Craig Carnelia
WALTER	Brad O'Hare
BIG JANE	Jane Galloway
LITTLE JANE	Maureen Silliman
K.C.	Karen Trott

The current version of *Three Postcards* (published here) received its premiere at Circle Repertory Company (Tanya Berezin, Artistic Director), in New York City on November 16, 1994. The direction and musical staging were by Tee Scatuorchio; the set design was by Derek McLane, the costume design was by Toni-Leslie James, the lighting design was by Tom Sturge, the music direction was by Steve Freeman, the dramaturg was Lynn M. Thomson and the stage manager was Denise Yaney. The cast was as follows:

BILL	Steve Freeman
WALTER	David Pittu
BIG JANE	Johanna Day
LITTLE JANE	Amy Kowallis
K.C.	Amanda Naughton

BILL, a piano player, thirties

WALTER, a waiter, late twenties, early thirties

BIG JANE, thirty to thirty-five

LITTLE JANE, thirty to thirty-five

K.C., thirty to thirty-five

■ PLACE ■

A Manhattan restaurant. The set may be as simple as a
grand piano and an oval table with three chairs.
This play is performed without an intermission.

■ MUSICAL NUMBERS ■

Opening	*All*
She Was K.C.	*Bill*
What the Song Should Say	*Big Jane, Little Jane, K.C.*
See How the Sun Shines (fragment)	*Big Jane, Little Jane, K.C.*
I've Been Watching You	*Walter, Bill, Little Jane*
Three Postcards	*Big Jane, Little Jane, K.C.*
The Picture in the Hall	*K.C.*
See How the Sun Shines	*Big Jane, Little Jane, K.C.*
A Minute	*Bill*
I'm Standing in This Room	*All*

In addition to the songs in *Three Postcards*, the musical score, played onstage at the piano by Bill, provides an almost continuous underscoring for the play. Nearly all the scenes taking place in the present are underscored with "restaurant music." A number of the scenes departing from the present reality have no music under them, while others do.

The intricate workings of this music, including all musical cues, can be found in the piano score (available from Dramatists Play Service, Inc.). We have attempted to keep the playscript relatively free of these notations.

Walter begins his preparations to open the restaurant. Big Jane enters and addresses the audience.

BIG JANE: I'd like to say something on behalf of my friends. I mean, you hear so much about marriage and families. Okay, yes, fine, every once in a while there is one of those female buddy movies where two women do actually seem to enjoy one another's company, brought together as they have been by the accidental murder of a potential rapist, and they ultimately decide that the only way for them both to be happy together is to drive off a cliff into, you know, a fiery, painful death, but . . . The great thing about having friends for such a long time, real friends, is there's nothing you can't talk about and there's nothing you have to talk about. You know?

(Little Jane enters, addresses the audience:)

LITTLE JANE: I think it's incredibly unusual for people to stay friends for a lifetime. It's so much easier to abandon a friend than it is a marriage or a child or parent. Those things take effort: lawyers, recriminations, strong force of will. But a friend you can walk away from in a second and no one can take you to court. You can kill off a whole friendship with nothing more lethal-seeming than a little indifference.

BIG JANE: Or just by changing, by marrying, and joining the invisible social club of parents who all, like, at the same exact instant shift their focus from careers and sex and adventure to . . . automobile safety features and nutrition.

(K.C. enters, addresses the audience:)

K.C.: When Little Jane called and said, "When are we gonna see you?" it seemed like April was far enough away it would never really come, and I'd have to feel better by then and it would be great to laugh and pretend we were fifteen again.

(Bill enters; he sits at the piano, begins to play.)

LITTLE JANE: Like anything worth having, friendship implies a commitment—to tell the truth and to work at it.

BIG JANE: She turns everything into a job.

LITTLE JANE: I mean, without struggle, there's no reward. You have to fight for and through and all the way around the things you care about.

K.C.: But then I remembered what she would be like.

LITTLE JANE: What is she trying to prove by being so remote? So perfect? Her mother died, for god's sake, it's okay to be sad, to be confused or angry. It's okay to be anything.

K.C.: It isn't okay with her that I'm okay. I'm supposed to be suffering, right?

LITTLE JANE: By saying: "Don't ask about that, don't go there, it should all be spontaneous and easy and magically free from strife," what she's really doing is defending herself against any real closeness.

(Walter sets the tables, lights candles, etc., while improvising a sung melody to Bill's playing.)

BIG JANE: K.C. was our inspiration: she wasn't afraid of anybody or anything. She was wild.

LITTLE JANE: Tonight we celebrate: after years, *years,* of my subtly dropping hint after hint, Big Jane has finally gone to a shrink.

BIG JANE: She just wants someone to share shrinkage with, I know that.

(Bill joins Walter, the two improvising a sung melody over the piano; at the same time:)

K.C.: Her whole life is therapy. Which would be fine if it had worked. You can't make a joke without her wanting to know what's behind the joke, what it reveals, what anger or anxiety or subverted rage it is fulfilling; I would rather eat glass than ask myself or anyone what a spontaneous joke reveals of their inner life: IT'S A JOKE!

LITTLE JANE: I love Big Jane, but it's been hard to see someone hurting themselves year after year.

BIG JANE: I love to go out and spend their money and drink wine and totally forget that there is anything outside the walls of that room.

K.C.: I mean, I loved my mom, but we didn't say it, we just knew it. She would have been uncomfortable if I'd told her I loved her.

LITTLE JANE: I mean, I love them both.

K.C.: She's also the kind of person who is always telling you she loves you. "We love you." What she means is, "Do you love me? Tell me you love me."

LITTLE JANE: But sometimes we just start giggling and squealing like we're still girls.

BIG JANE: They make me feel young.

LITTLE JANE: I hate it when one of us goes, "Yay! Yay!" And it's usually me!

BIG JANE: We were "The Three Tramps."

LITTLE JANE AND K.C.: Back then . . .
BIG JANE, LITTLE JANE AND K.C.: We were everything.
BIG JANE: We didn't need anybody.
LITTLE JANE: We could do anything.
K.C.: We were ridiculous.

(All five characters look out front, and they sing together for the first time—a low, sustained note, wordless. Walter puts the final touches on the restaurant, completing the picture, as the music ends. He then pats his hair and checks the specials as K.C. and Little Jane exit. Walter moves to unlock the front door of the restaurant.)

WALTER *(To Bill)*: Showtime!

(And Big Jane is there. The music from the piano snaps into that of an appropriately subdued restaurant ambience.)

BIG JANE: Hi.
WALTER: Good evening. Reservation?
BIG JANE: I hope so.
WALTER: For?
BIG JANE: Three, please?
WALTER: Your name?
BIG JANE: Oh. Ingham.

(Walter looks in the reservation book.)

But I didn't make it. Um, Fleischman? . . . Or Kissel? I'm sorry, I don't know who made it, I don't know anything . . .
WALTER: Right this way, please.
BIG JANE: Thank you. Oh, this is beautiful! God. How long have you been open?
WALTER: Fifteen years.
BIG JANE: Oh wow. *Really?*
WALTER: May I hang up your coat?

BIG JANE: No, that's all right, I may have to make a quick get-away. Thanks.

WALTER: Something to drink?

BIG JANE: Ohhhhh, yeah, I'll have . . . What's good? I'm a grown-up! I'll have a white wine. Straight up. Please, thank you. Very much. I promise not to be a problem. From here on out. *(As Walter starts to move away)* Oh, you have a piano player, too! Nothing, sorry.

(Walter continues off. Pause. Little Jane enters.)

WALTER: Good evening. Reservation—?

LITTLE JANE: I see my friend, thank you. *(She moves toward the table)*

BIG JANE: Hi, Jane.

LITTLE JANE: Hi, Jane.

BIG JANE: Hi, hi, hi.

LITTLE JANE: Hi.

BIG JANE: How are you?

LITTLE JANE: You look great.

BIG JANE: So do you.

LITTLE JANE: Ugh.

BIG JANE: You do.

(Walter arrives beside them.)

WALTER: Would you like me to hang up your coat?

LITTLE JANE: Oh. Sure. *(To Big Jane)* You want a cocktail?

BIG JANE: I ordered.

LITTLE JANE: Already? Okay. I'll . . .

BIG JANE: Why do they call it a cocktail? You know? Cock. Tail. Doesn't that seem weird?

LITTLE JANE: I'm ignoring her and you should, too . . . I'll have a dry Rob Roy on the rocks with a cherry on top.

(Walter continues off as:)

BIG JANE: That's great, thanks. Sorry about the—never mind!

(Walter is off.)

LITTLE JANE: So? How was it?

BIG JANE: What? Oh. I didn't go.

LITTLE JANE: Oh, you're kidding.

BIG JANE: No. But I had a job! I mean an interview. But I'm seeing him Tuesday. I am!

LITTLE JANE: What was the job?

BIG JANE: Don't be that way.

LITTLE JANE: It's your decision, go or don't go. What was the job?

BIG JANE: I had to move the appointment to Tuesday.

LITTLE JANE: Great.

BIG JANE: I'm seeing him, I am.

LITTLE JANE: What was the job?, it's fine, Jane.

BIG JANE: Oh just, you know, nothing, phone sales, it's horrible.

LITTLE JANE: Why?

BIG JANE: No, it's fine, I can work out of the apartment, I can make my own hours, you don't need experience.

LITTLE JANE: Sounds great. What's it pay?

BIG JANE: Oh, please. But—how's Bob?

LITTLE JANE: Diversionary tactic. He's fine.

BIG JANE: He is?

LITTLE JANE: No, he's not, he's the same, but . . . Or maybe he's better, I can't tell, I'd be the last to know, probably, since I'm married to him.

BIG JANE: Uh-huh.

LITTLE JANE: You know? Let me . . . I'll wait and we'll talk about it when K.C. gets here. Is that okay?

BIG JANE: Sure.

LITTLE JANE: I just . . . I want to talk about it, but I spent my whole session talking about it this morning—

BIG JANE: Uh-huh.

LITTLE JANE: —and I'm still a little . . . Is that okay?

BIG JANE: Sure.

LITTLE JANE: You sure? . . . So did he charge you? For canceling?

BIG JANE: Bob? Oh. No. Should he?

(Pause. Walter arrives with drinks.)

Hello again.

LITTLE JANE: Could we look at a wine list while we're waiting for our friend?

BIG JANE: This whole place is really beautiful. Thank you.

(Walter moves off.)

He hates me. Cheers.

LITTLE JANE: Cheers.

(They sip their drinks.)

BIG JANE: What's the matter? Is it bad? Send it back.

LITTLE JANE: It's fine. How's the writing? You submitted anything?

BIG JANE: No, I haven't, but . . .

LITTLE JANE: You're working on stuff?

BIG JANE: Yeah. So—

LITTLE JANE: Good.

(Big Jane shrugs: "Who knows?" Short pause.)

Oh, the other thing? When you see the shrink? I mean,
you know, if you go.

BIG JANE: I'm seeing him Tuesday.

LITTLE JANE: Is, you just, you start remembering all this *stuff.*

BIG JANE: Uh-huh?

LITTLE JANE: I remembered this one thing, right like in the
first week or something, I'd barely hit the couch . . .

BIG JANE: Is this . . . ?

LITTLE JANE: What? . . .

(Big Jane shakes her head: "Go ahead.")

What?

BIG JANE: No. Go ahead. I thought maybe you'd told me this.

LITTLE JANE: I don't think I told this to anybody but Bob. And Dr. Cindy.

BIG JANE: Okay.

LITTLE JANE: No, I'm sure I didn't. What did you think it was?

BIG JANE: Well . . . The thing about your brother and the pencil? . . . It is?!? Oh, I love that.

LITTLE JANE: No, I just . . . What time is it, do you know?

BIG JANE: Oh, tell it.

LITTLE JANE: I think . . . What time do you have?

BIG JANE: I flushed my watch down the toilet. I don't want to talk about it, it was horrible. Tell the pencil story. Please?

LITTLE JANE: Have you talked to K.C.?

BIG JANE *("No")*: Uh-uhn. Tell the pencil story.

LITTLE JANE: I did.

BIG JANE: You did.

LITTLE JANE: Yesterday.

BIG JANE: And?

LITTLE JANE: You know. She's Case.

BIG JANE: Uh-huh. So, okay, you walk in, your parents are naked, you and your brother Larry are there—

LITTLE JANE: No. I'll—okay, here, I'll tell you something else I remembered—

BIG JANE: Okay.

LITTLE JANE: But this one isn't funny.

BIG JANE: Okay.

LITTLE JANE: The thing about the room? Did I tell you this?

BIG JANE: What room?

LITTLE JANE: Well . . . There's just this . . . it's just this *image.* There's no punch line to this.

BIG JANE: Okay.

LITTLE JANE: I'm standing in this room, I'm like three, maybe, or younger or I don't know . . .

BIG JANE: Uh-huh?

LITTLE JANE: Annnnd . . . Are you sure I didn't tell you—? Okay: I don't know if we've just moved in or they've just painted or something but . . . there's no furniture—

BIG JANE: Uh-huh.

LITTLE JANE: —and I'm not looking at anything in particular . . . I'm just . . . standing there . . . and I have
this . . . very intense . . . experience . . .

*(A momentary silence from the piano; Little Jane is unable
to find the right words; the music resumes.)*

It's like . . . it's as if I understand my whole existence
or something.
BIG JANE: Yes.
LITTLE JANE: But it's *not* that.
BIG JANE: Oh.

*(During the following, Walter arrives with the wine list and
menus, Little Jane does not acknowledge him; Big Jane
mouths, "Thank you" as Walter retreats.)*

LITTLE JANE: I mean . . . it changes . . . whenever I try to
describe it, it's like . . . I get this close . . .
BIG JANE: Yes.
LITTLE JANE: And I feel it's something I have to get back to.
But if I start to close in on it . . . *(Remembering some-
thing)* Oh! OH! Did you see that thing in the paper
about the particles? . . . The subatomic particles?
BIG JANE: Uhn-un.
LITTLE JANE: Oh—

(K.C. enters. Walter greets her at the door.)

BIG JANE: There she is!

*(The action becomes silent slow-motion. Little Jane waves to
K.C., who waves back. All-around beaming as Walter takes
K.C.'s coat. Through this, a spot of light isolates Little Jane
and Big Jane, and we hear their thoughts, sung by Bill:)*

BILL:

She was K.C. at seven.
She was K.C. at ten.

And at eighteen and thirty,
She was K.C. again.

And I wondered at seven,
And I wondered at ten,
And I wondered at eighteen
And at thirty again.

Always under the smile
I wonder how K.C. sees me.
Always under the smile
I wonder if K.C. sees me.

She's got another great haircut there.

(The action returns to real time as K.C. reaches the table.)

K.C.: Hi!

BIG JANE: Hiiiiii!

LITTLE JANE: Hi.

K.C.: Don't get my cold.

LITTLE JANE: Ohhh, you're kidding.

K.C.: It's just starting, I think.

LITTLE JANE: Oh, well, you're no longer contagious then.

BIG JANE: You look fantastic.

LITTLE JANE: It's only before you really know you have it that you're actually contagious.

K.C.: Thank you, Doctor.

BIG JANE: You do, you look incredible.

LITTLE JANE: Doesn't she?

K.C.: Thanks.

LITTLE JANE: I love your hair.

BIG JANE: Me, too.

LITTLE JANE: Yay!

BIG JANE: Yay, yay!

K.C. *(To Big Jane)*: So?	LITTLE JANE *(To K.C.)*: So how are you?

K.C.: Good.

LITTLE JANE: Good. Are you sure? . . . You really look . . .

BIG JANE: You do.

K.C.: This is nice.

BIG JANE: Isn't it?

LITTLE JANE: Isn't it? Bob's eaten here, and he says the something . . . oh, what was it? . . . the something is fantastic.

K.C.: Well, I'll be sure to have something.

LITTLE JANE: Some sort of . . . seafood, I think.

BIG JANE *(To K.C.)*: HI!!!!

K.C.: Hi. Of course, I forgot my umbrella, so . . .

BIG JANE: What, is it raining?	LITTLE JANE: Let's—okay let's get you a drink. Hello-oh!

K.C.: No, but it looks like it's going to, so . . . we can all look bad soon again.

(Little Jane tries to get Walter's attention; he is busy elsewhere.)

BIG JANE: Yay!

K.C.: So? How'd it go?

BIG JANE: What? Oh—

LITTLE JANE: She didn't go.

BIG JANE: No.

LITTLE JANE: But she got a job!	K.C.: Oh.

BIG JANE: Sort of.

K.C.: Oh, great, what is it?

BIG JANE: It's shit.

LITTLE JANE: No, come on—

BIG JANE: It's, you know, it's nothing, it's phone sales.

LITTLE JANE: It's great.

BIG JANE: Magazines.

LITTLE JANE: It's gonna pay the bills, right? So—

(Walter comes over to them.)

Our friend would like something to drink, please.

K.C.: And what would she like? No, seriously, I don't know what to have. What are you having? *(She reaches for Little Jane's glass)*

LITTLE JANE: No, you don't want this. You want me to order for you?

K.C.: Mm-hm.

LITTLE JANE: You're sure?

K.C. *(Sotto voce to Big Jane)*: She loves this.

LITTLE JANE: What? I don't care what you're saying about me, um . . . you like Lillet?

K.C.: Mm-hm.

LITTLE JANE: You sure?

(Again Little Jane prevents K.C. from checking out her drink.)

It's a Rob Roy, you don't want it—we'll take two Lillets on the rocks with a twist of orange, please. *(To K.C.)* Okay?

K.C.: That's great.

(Walter takes back the Rob Roy, but Big Jane intercepts it behind Little Jane's back. She sips it as Walter moves off.)

BIG JANE *(To K.C.)*: So did you drive?

K.C. *("No")*: Mm-mm.

BIG JANE: Train?

K.C. *("Yes")*: Mm-hm.

Little Jane: Was it crowded?

(K.C. shakes her head no.)

How's Leo?

K.C.: He's good. He's still really busy, but that's good, too.

LITTLE JANE: Good.

BIG JANE: And the girls?

K.C.: Everybody's okay.

LITTLE JANE: Great.

BIG JANE: Great.

LITTLE JANE: Do they . . . Is it . . . I mean, is it harder with them being so young? I know this must be like twenty questions—

K.C.: It's really been okay. I really feel okay. I do.

LITTLE JANE: Great. *(Brief pause)* We believe you!

BIG JANE: We believe you.

LITTLE JANE: We just want to make sure, that's all. We love you.

(K.C. smiles back; short pause.)

BIG JANE: How's the puppy, is he cute?

K.C.: Mm-hm.

LITTLE JANE: He is?

K.C.: Oh, yeah. He's totally adorable. He's so happy just to be alive.

BIG JANE: Ohhhh.   LITTLE JANE: That's great.

K.C.: The rug, my feet, everything, it's all cause for celebration: "Oh look, wow! WOW!, look what I found: a piece of dirty *wood*!"

LITTLE JANE: How 'bout your dad?

K.C.: He likes my dad.

LITTLE JANE: No, how's   K.C.: No, he's great, he's
he—?   doing fine.

LITTLE JANE: He is. That's good.

BIG JANE: Good.

K.C.: You know. He's up and down . . .

LITTLE JANE: Oh sure.

K.C.: But . . .

LITTLE JANE: Give him time.

K.C.: He's really fine.

LITTLE JANE: It's hard.

BIG JANE: Oh yeah.

LITTLE JANE: It has to be . . . He has to be going through so much. Even if he can't necessarily articulate it all.

(Beat.)

K.C.: This is very nice.

BIG JANE: Isn't it? *(Pause)* It's beautiful.

LITTLE JANE: I like the glass.

BIG JANE: Me, too. *(Pause)* It's great to see you.

(K.C. smiles. Small pause.)

LITTLE JANE: It really is.

(K.C. still smiles, then looks down at the table. Substantial pause. They sing:)

BIG JANE, LITTLE JANE AND K.C.:
The song should say . . . a restaurant.
The song should say . . . an evening.
And in the words, a chance of rain,
A table and three chairs.

The song should have city sounds,
Far away and fast.
And as it flows the song should have
The waiter brushing past.
And it should say a piano plays
All the evening long,
And we should be . . . in the song.

Father, mother, brother, naked.
How's the puppy? Did you drive?
Tuesday, thank you, my umbrella.
Just to be alive.
And in the song the room should fill,
    the room should fill,
Day should turn to night.
    Night should fall.
Conversations overheard,
    voices from the bar,
Laughter out of sight.
    Happy Birthday.
Other tables,
    other lives,
Other chairs,
    smoke drifting by.
All of them belong.
And we should be . . .

Running and reaching
And chasing the song as it goes,
Getting closer,
And finding we're lost in the song as it grows . . .

K.C.:	LITTLE JANE:	BIG JANE:
Finding . . .	Finding . . .	Finding . . .
Father, mother	I'm very young.	Husbands,
In the fall.	I'm very small.	Lovers
Father, mother	And I'm standing,	
In the chill.	Standing still.	In the song.
Father, mother	And I understand	Young
In the hall,	Everything.	Girls
Standing	Standing	Dancing,
perfectly,	perfectly,	Dancing,
Perfectly still.	Perfectly still.	Dancing
		In each other's arms
		In the song.

BIG JANE, LITTLE JANE AND K.C.:
> The song should say
> Three friends in a restaurant.
> The song should say
> An April evening.
>> Night should fall.
> And in the words,
>> hidden in the words,
> A chance of rain,
> A chance of anything at all.
> The song should say a piano plays
> All the evening long.
>> All night long.

> *(Pause.)*

> But there should be more.
> Somehow . . .
> Somehow the music should soar,
> And so should we.
> We should soar in the song
>> somehow . . . perfectly . . .
> We should be . . . should be carried along,
>> carried along
> By the song.
>> On and on and on and on and
>> on and on and on and on . . .

> *(Restaurant music restores.)*

BIG JANE: Oh, tell the pencil story!

LITTLE JANE *(Looks at Big Jane, then to K.C.)*: Oh, did you see this thing in the paper about the subatomic particles?

K.C. *("No")*: Mm-mm.   BIG JANE: Please?

LITTLE JANE: I was telling Jane before you came, there was this thing about these, I don't know what they're called, little tiny particles, infinitesimal—

K.C.: Uh-huh.

LITTLE JANE: Which apparently move one way when they're not being observed, don't ask me how they know that, and then change what they do when they know they're being watched. Isn't that incredible?

K.C.: Why?

LITTLE JANE: The act of observing them literally changes, I guess, the nature of . . . the act.

K.C.: Well, it's certainly true of sex.

BIG JANE: Mm-hm.

K.C.: I hate it when people are standing around watching, don't you?

BIG JANE: Tell the pencil story. Please, Little Jane?

LITTLE JANE: She's heard the pencil story.

K.C.: What pencil story?

BIG JANE: See?

LITTLE JANE: Everyone, people in New Zealand have heard the pencil story.

BIG JANE: She hasn't. Pretty please, with sprinkles?

LITTLE JANE: Someday, when God is looking around for someone to punish . . .

K.C.: You know she's dying to tell it.

LITTLE JANE: You've heard this; I know you have.

K.C.: I don't remember.

BIG JANE: Please?

LITTLE JANE: My brother Larry and I were like—

BIG JANE: Yay!

LITTLE JANE: And I meant what I said, God is watching. I don't know, four maybe, five? And it was New Year's Day, just stop me if this starts to sound familiar, and we get up and the house is really quiet, so like good children we make an incredible racket trying to wake our parents and . . . nothing, you know. So finally we knock on their door: still nothing. We tiptoe in.

BIG JANE: They're hungover.

LITTLE JANE: And there they are: stark naked. And, I mean, it's kind of like watching a spider eat a fly, you can't really take your eyes off it . . . so, but we cough, you know, and . . . we sit on the bed, we bounce: they're dead to the world. And . . . I don't remember whose idea this was, but— . . . *one* of us picked up this pencil off the nightstand and . . . we started poking them with it . . . the eraser end—

K.C.: How old were you?

BIG JANE: Twenty.

LITTLE JANE: And we're poking, and to this day I honestly cannot tell you which one of us did this but— . . . *one* of us . . . gently . . . inserts the eraser . . .

BIG JANE: Into—

LITTLE JANE: Into our dad's—

(Walter arrives with the two Lillets.)

BIG JANE: Hello!

WALTER: Would you like to hear the specials?

LITTLE JANE: Only if I can ruin them as effectively as you just ruined my story.

WALTER: Oh.

LITTLE JANE: Go ahead, I'll stand behind you and hover, distracting everyone's attention.

WALTER: Sorry.

LITTLE JANE: No, actually I think we want a little more time just to visit before we think about food—okay?

(K.C. and Big Jane concur.)

(To Walter) Thanks.

BIG JANE: I'll take another white wine when you get a chance. No hurry. Thanks.

(He moves off.)

LITTLE JANE: God.

BIG JANE: Anyway. Go ahead.

LITTLE JANE: Anyway, so there it is . . . We've let go. It's freestanding at this point.

K.C.: Uh-huh?

LITTLE JANE: And they *still do not wake up*! And . . . we look at one another and realize in the same second we've probably transgressed some invisible law . . .

K.C.: Thou shalt not violate thy father's crack.

BIG JANE: Right.

LITTLE JANE: And we sneak back out and wait for them to get up. And out they stumble. You know. And . . . no one . . . ever . . . says . . . anything!

BIG JANE: AAAAAAAAAA!

LITTLE JANE: Ever.

BIG JANE: He wakes up with the pencil—

K.C.: Right.

BIG JANE: —in his butt—

LITTLE JANE: What does he think?

BIG JANE: "How much did I drink? Was it my wife?"

LITTLE JANE: "Was I sleepwalking? Was my asshole trying to do a crossword puzzle?"

BIG JANE: Really! And you can't ask your kids, "Did either of you happen to leave a pencil sticking out of my butt?"

LITTLE JANE: Not really.

K.C.: Yes. I had heard that.

LITTLE JANE: What?

K.C.: I had heard that story. It's very funny!

BIG JANE: Save me, help! Waiter!

(Walter returns with Big Jane's wine.)

We're ready for the specials, I think.

WALTER: Okay.

BIG JANE: Don't you love that, though? I love that story.

WALTER: For appetizers tonight:

BIG JANE: Oh boy. Sorry.

WALTER: The soup is a cream of fennel; and we have our seafood mousse—

LITTLE JANE: *That's* it.

WALTER: —with a light champagne sauce topped with mushroom caps and fried grapes.

K.C.: Grapes?

WALTER: That's excellent. And the frog's legs *Provençal*. Our entrées include two veal dishes tonight: a St. Gallen veal sausage with rosti potatoes and braised onions and a grilled *paillard* of veal with caper butter. We have fresh Cornish hen stuffed with pine nuts, raisins and Bulgar wheat.

BIG JANE: Uh!

WALTER: A green peppercorn steak, flambéed with cognac. And for the fish we have red snapper prepared very simply—*meunière*, with snail-braised leeks on the side.

LITTLE JANE: Did . . . the snails actually do the braising? Or . . . ?

WALTER: We also have a roast duck with cherries and a Grand Marnier sauce. And our lobster with cider sauce and baby vegetables.

BIG JANE: Ohhh, baby vegetables!

(As Walter is already moving away:)

LITTLE JANE: Could I have more water, please?

BIG JANE: I wish I had that on videotape, though.

K.C.: A lot of fruit and liquor is all I can tell you.

LITTLE JANE: Snail-braised leeks, I love it.

BIG JANE: Oh yeah, I didn't get that.

LITTLE JANE: He said they were serving fish with snail-braised leeks. And I said, Did the snails do the braising?

BIG JANE *(Not comprehending)*: Uh-huh?

LITTLE JANE: He meant the leeks had been braised *with* snails. If something is man-made . . . or home-grown—

BIG JANE *(Still not getting it)*: Ohhhh.

LITTLE JANE: This is my treat, by the way.

BIG JANE: Nooooo!

LITTLE JANE: Yesssss!

BIG JANE: Thank you. So . . .

K.C.: How's Seth?

LITTLE JANE: Good. I think we're going to let him do another year of kindergarten.

K.C.: You are.

LITTLE JANE: Yeah. I don't know.

K.C.: I think that's smart.

LITTLE JANE: I can't . . . Yeah, I think it is. But . . .

(Walter returns with the pitcher of water. He fills Little Jane's glass.)

K.C.: How's Bob?

(Little Jane is looking up at Walter.)

WALTER *(Directly to Little Jane)*: I hate you.

LITTLE JANE *(No reaction)*: Thanks. *(To K.C.)* He's the same. He's, I mean, maybe *he's* why Seth is acting this way, who knows.

K.C.: His . . . ?

LITTLE JANE: Bob's drinking. Yeah. Or not. I mean, maybe it's just biochemical.

BIG JANE: All kids run around and make too much noise. Don't they?

LITTLE JANE: Maybe it's, I mean, the girls never really had this kind of problem, did they? Where they bite everybody who comes in the house? God. So, I feel like, I mean, just as my brother and I were probably trying to tell my father *something* with the pencil, and we were about the same age Seth is now, maybe he's trying to get our attention. Maybe he senses the tension between us, and how much of the time Bob is actually out of it or seems—whatever a five year old can sense—

K.C.: Uh-huh.

LITTLE JANE: —and he acts more like a child.

BIG JANE: He's five years old. He's supposed to act like a child.

LITTLE JANE: Cindy wants me to do an intervention, because he was sort of, not sort of, he was *weird* on his birthday, but . . . honestly, I just . . . I don't think it's *that* bad. Do you?

BIG JANE: He's five years old.

LITTLE JANE: I'm talking about Bob now, Jane.

BIG JANE: I know.

LITTLE JANE: So anyway, I don't know . . . What shall we drink? Is white all right?

BIG JANE: Sure.

LITTLE JANE: What's everybody eating? Sorry.

BIG JANE: What are you gonna have?

K.C.: I'm either . . . I haven't really . . .

LITTLE JANE: Have the duck. I don't want it, but I want to taste it. I'm gonna have the mousse, and the veal. I think.

BIG JANE: What was the one . . . with the Bulgar wheat and the flambé of something? *(Pause)* What looks good to you?

K.C.: You two order, I'll decide.

LITTLE JANE: No, we'll wait.

K.C.: No, it'll force me to make up my mind.

LITTLE JANE: You sure? You know what you want?

BIG JANE: I just have to ask him something.

LITTLE JANE *(Motioning Walter over)*: I think . . .

(Walter approaches.)

WALTER: All set?

LITTLE JANE: I'll—

BIG JANE: What— *(To Little Jane)* I'm sorry. *(To Walter)* What was the one with the Bulgar wheat? And the flambé?—

WALTER: The Cornish hen? It's not flambéed.

BIG JANE: Oh. Well . . .

LITTLE JANE: You want that?

BIG JANE: I'll have that.

WALTER: Appetizer?

BIG JANE: No, thank you.

LITTLE JANE: You sure? It's on me. I'm going to have the seafood mousse. And the veal.

WALTER: Sausage?

LITTLE JANE: No, the *paillard?*

BIG JANE: How do you know these words?

LITTLE JANE: And we'll take a bottle of the *Chassagne-Montrachet*, thank you. A *paillard* is like a flattened . . . thing.

K.C.: Oh god . . . I'll . . .

LITTLE JANE: Have the duck.

K.C.: I'llllllllllllll . . .

LITTLE JANE: The duck! The duck!

BIG JANE: Try the duck.

LITTLE JANE: We want the duck!

BIG JANE: Try it. Take the duck!

LITTLE JANE: The duck!

BIG JANE: Duck!

K.C.: I'll have the duck.

BIG JANE: Yay!

LITTLE JANE: One duck coming right up!

K.C.: And a cup of the soup.

WALTER: It only comes in a bowl.

K.C.: Fine.

LITTLE JANE: You're not going to regret that duck, I promise.

(Walter starts to move off.)

BIG JANE: Thanks!

K.C.: Do you ever hear from the airline steward?

BIG JANE: No—but oh, I heard from Tommy!

K.C.: You did.

BIG JANE: Yeah. He's terrific.

K.C.: Uh-huh.

BIG JANE: And he's still with Mark. And they seem really happy. And they want me to clean their apartment. You know. So . . .

K.C.: What do you mean?

BIG JANE: Anyway, just for a little extra cash, I said I needed money, who knows?

K.C.: Is that wise?

BIG JANE: I mean, how long has it been? I'm not in love with him anymore. It's a job.

K.C.: You're going to clean the apartment of your ex-boyfriend? And his boyfriend?

BIG JANE: Only if I want to. Why shouldn't I?

K.C.: Well, see, here in America, the idea of getting down on our knees and cleaning out the toilet bowl we used to use when we were in love with the guy who left us for another man—

BIG JANE: I knew he was bisexual.

K.C.: *Still,* there are those who would say that to accept the position at all is in some small way to make a putz out of one's own nose. Don't do it. I will pay you not to do it.

(Walter arrives with the wine, which he presents to Little Jane; she gives him a tiny nod, and he begins to uncork the bottle.)

BIG JANE: Okay.

K.C.: All right?

BIG JANE: I'm not going to.

K.C.: Are you positive?

BIG JANE: Yes.

K.C.: Good.

LITTLE JANE: Good.

(As the cork pops from the bottle, K.C., Little Jane and Bill all freeze, and the music abruptly ends.
Lights change. Walter addresses Big Jane, assuming the bipartisan tone of a psychotherapist.)

WALTER: How'd that make you feel?

BIG JANE: What do you mean?

WALTER: When they spoke to you that way, how did you feel?

BIG JANE: Well, they're my friends, I mean, they're just saying don't let people run over you, that's all.

WALTER: Is that what you think you're doing?

(She shakes her head no.)

So why didn't you say that?

BIG JANE: Because then I didn't have to get into, you know, the whole thing.

WALTER: No. What whole—?

BIG JANE: Well . . . the fact that I already cleaned his apartment.

WALTER: You did.

BIG JANE: But that's not really the problem.

WALTER: What's the problem?

BIG JANE: I guess . . . I don't really feel like I need to be in therapy with you just now.

LITTLE JANE *(Unfreezes)*: Oh please. Are you kidding?

BIG JANE: This is my session!

(Little Jane agrees to stop talking.)

I'm not the same person I used to be. She treats me like I'm still fourteen, and I'm not . . .

WALTER *(To Little Jane)*: Is that true? Is that what you do?

BIG JANE: This is—Hey!

LITTLE JANE: How can we even be having this discussion about her feelings when she doesn't know what they are?

BIG JANE: I'm canceling Tuesday if this is the way it's going to be.

WALTER: Is that how you get what you want? By threatening to hurt yourself?

LITTLE JANE: Yes! I mean, and she won't *explore*. She's threatened by the idea of finding out who she is and it's why she's stuck where she is. I'm sorry, but . . . honestly, at your age, it's getting sad, Jane.

WALTER: Do you feel that?

BIG JANE: . . . No.

LITTLE JANE: This is really very . . . painful to have to say . . .

BIG JANE: What?

LITTLE JANE: Your poetry stinks.

BIG JANE: . . . It does?

LITTLE JANE: I brought along some corroboration.

K.C. *(Unfreezes)*: We don't like having to do this any more than you like having to listen. But it's in your best interest, Jane.

BIG JANE: What is this, an *intervention*? Please, you don't need to do this—

K.C.: I quote: "I turn to face the sea—"

BIG JANE: Please, please, you're right, I hate that poem.

K.C.: "The foam sparkles against my skin like—"

LITTLE JANE AND K.C.: "—tiny ping-pong balls."

BIG JANE: That's why I never make any submissions, I'm still not good enough.

LITTLE JANE AND K.C.: "Why?, I ask the crashing drum of water at my feet—"

BIG JANE: That's an old poem, stop!

LITTLE JANE AND K.C. *(Overlapping)*: "Why does all this have to be? The needless pain—"

BIG JANE: STOP, *STOP*, PLEASE!

K.C. *(Gently)*: You're never going to be good enough.

BIG JANE: You don't know that.

LITTLE JANE: You don't have the vocabulary to be a writer. You're thirty-three years old, you have no discernible skills except your extraordinary gift for making people feel good—

BIG JANE: Well, that's something.

LITTLE JANE: Yes, it is.

K.C.: It's a lot. But . . . you don't know when to pay your income tax—

BIG JANE: That's true.

K.C.: You've had seventeen boyfriends in two years.

LITTLE JANE: You don't know how to drive a car—

BIG JANE: All true—

K.C.: Or keep an apartment or a job as a waitress—

LITTLE JANE: You have to at *least* know the names of the food-stuffs: "Is *that* a scallop!"

BIG JANE *(To Walter)*: We never had them.

WALTER: Why is it so important to you both that she be something other than she is?

BIG JANE: Yes. Thank you. That's a very good point.	LITTLE JANE *(To Walter)*: Wait. All right? Once—wait, wait . . . Please. Once you hear this I think you'll understand.

BIG JANE: Oh, don't let's go into all—

LITTLE JANE: Seven years ago:

BIG JANE: It's ancient history—

K.C. *(Overlapping)*: Yes. Okay. We decided that Big Jane needed a vacation.

LITTLE JANE: She doesn't have a job and she's just broken up with, I can't remember . . .

BIG JANE: Marco.

LITTLE JANE: Marco.

K.C.: Is he the one who gave you herpes?

BIG JANE: No. That was—   LITTLE JANE: Gino.

K.C.: Right, right. *("Big difference")* Gino, Marco.

LITTLE JANE: So we agree to put up the money for her to take ten carefree days in—

LITTLE JANE AND K.C.: Martinique.

K.C. *(To Walter)*: Have you ever been to Martinique?

BIG JANE: It's very nice.

K.C.: Who would know?

LITTLE JANE: Really. So we agree to pick up the mail and water the plants—

K.C.: —feed the cat—

LITTLE JANE: The cat! Because what's ten days?

K.C.: Five years.

LITTLE JANE: Five.

WALTER: You sound as if you weren't pleased for her. Why wouldn't you want your good friend to be in a nice place?

BIG JANE: My point. Exactly. You're *great.*

LITTLE JANE: Well, after we learn that we're not really welcome to come visit her in Martinique—

BIG JANE: No, come on—

LITTLE JANE: —because our best friend's boyfriend—please, I don't care to hear his name right now.

BIG JANE: Creep.

K.C.: Lizard-like.   LITTLE JANE: Has a small jealous streak, but I quote, "He's really very nice, except that—"

BIG JANE: He hit me.

LITTLE JANE AND K.C.: He hit her.

LITTLE JANE: And got her pregnant—

BIG JANE: Well, that was partly my doing.

LITTLE JANE: —and disappeared altogether.

K.C.: Then skipped town. But really it was no trouble contacting the American consulate—

LITTLE JANE: No.

K.C.: And our congressman—because you had no passport—

BIG JANE: That's right.   LITTLE JANE: No, no.

K.C.: —and paying for the flight back—

LITTLE JANE: Then the abortion.

K.C.: And the cat's operation.

LITTLE JANE: Right.

K.C.: And the little kitty funeral urn.

LITTLE JANE: Ohhhh.

BIG JANE: And my landlord was suing you. Wasn't he? Oh god.

LITTLE JANE *(Overlapping)*: Oh, right, right, her landlord *was* suing me, because I had to co-sign, of course—

BIG JANE: This was awful.

LITTLE JANE *(Continuous)*: —on the sublease and the new tenant turned out to be:

BIG JANE, LITTLE JANE AND K.C.: A heroin addict.

LITTLE JANE: But none of that mattered. Finally.

K.C.: It didn't.

BIG JANE: Oh good.

LITTLE JANE: It really didn't. It was just the feeling that you weren't really our friend.

K.C.: That you really didn't care about us.

LITTLE JANE: That was the worst part. That getting shtupped by some phony-French lowlife was more important than either of our feelings for you.

WALTER: Why do you think you did those things?

(A beat.
Lights and restaurant music restore. Little Jane tastes the wine.)

LITTLE JANE: Fine, thank you.

(Walter pours.)

(To Big Jane) What?
BIG JANE: No, I was just thinking, I love your hair like that.
LITTLE JANE: Thanks. I've worn it like this for years.
BIG JANE: I know. But it still looks good.
LITTLE JANE: Thanks.
BIG JANE: Cheers.
K.C.: Cheers.
LITTLE JANE: Cheers.

(They raise their glasses. Walter lights the candle on their table as restaurant music concludes.
All the other lights onstage fade out, and the three of them are suddenly alone in the candlelight; they have become teenagers. K.C. and Big Jane do a makeover on Little Jane throughout:)

BIG JANE: He's a shit! You know? How he could say that to you!
LITTLE JANE: I'm *fine,* I don't need you to do this for me, guys, really.
K.C.: I want to try these new colors, and I can't see them on my own face, all right?

(Pause.)

LITTLE JANE: You probably think I look like a tramp, too, right?
K.C.: Yes, now shut up and let me do this before I stop having so much fun and have to just like . . . I don't know . . . do *something.*
BIG JANE: Oooooo, big threat.

(Pause. K.C. works in silence for a moment. A rumble of thunder from the piano.)

I love electrical storms.

K.C.: Me, too.

BIG JANE: I love blackouts. It's like the nineteenth century or something. I love when like the whole town is in complete darkness, the Russians could invade and we wouldn't even know about it, you know?

K.C.: Yeah, that'd be *great. (Looks at the color she has just applied)* Too pale.

(Short pause.)

BIG JANE: You want to come stay at my house, Jane, you can.

K.C.: Or mine.

BIG JANE: Oh, her house is nicer.

LITTLE JANE: True. No offense.

BIG JANE: Let's stay there.

K.C.: Close your eyes.

LITTLE JANE *(To K.C.)*: Sometimes I still can't even believe you're our friend.

K.C.: I'm just really glad you called us, I mean it—

BIG JANE: Me, too.

K.C.: The minute he started getting weird.

LITTLE JANE: He was born weird.

BIG JANE: Why doesn't your mom just tell him to go to bed or something?

LITTLE JANE: Oh, who knows what her problem is, she just stands there with that dumb look on her face: "What, me worry?" She lets him get away with murder.

K.C.: I bet he has a really little dick. I do, I feel it.

BIG JANE: You *feel* it?

LITTLE JANE: I'm fine about it, let's just—

BIG JANE: Let's not talk about it.

K.C.: Really, it's a deal.

LITTLE JANE: I can't even believe we actually conceded to playing Monopoly with that stupid fuck—

BIG JANE: Forget it. *(Short pause)* I mean, then he just turns and asks, "Does anybody *else* think my daughter looks like a tramp?"

LITTLE JANE: We were there, Jane.

K.C.: I thought we weren't gonna talk about it.

BIG JANE: Okay, I didn't bring it—

LITTLE JANE: We don't need an instant replay.

BIG JANE: *You* brought it up again, I didn't.

LITTLE JANE: *(Pause; to herself)* Soused-up fatso . . .

BIG JANE: STOP TALKING ABOUT IT!

K.C.: This color is so much better.

LITTLE JANE: Is there anything in there that'll make me look like you? I'm serious.

K.C.: You're beautiful, Jane.

LITTLE JANE: I just want to be both of you sometimes.

BIG JANE: Maybe you *are*. No, maybe she is! Did you ever think that?

K.C.: No.

BIG JANE: No, maybe it just seems like you're over there and I'm over here: like it *seems* that the sun goes around the earth. Maybe we're the same person. *(Pause)* Right? Or maybe not.

K.C. *(Sips her wine)*: This is really delicious. Isn't it?

BIG JANE: Isn't it?

LITTLE JANE *(Mimicking her)*: "Isn't it?"

BIG JANE: "Isn't it?"

K.C.: Okay.

(She turns Little Jane toward Big Jane.)

BIG JANE: Great. You look great.

K.C.: That's better, right?

LITTLE JANE: Thanks. A lot.

(K.C. presses the lipstick into Little Jane's palm.)

K.C.: Keep this. It's much better on you than me.

(A loud knock from the darkness.)

WALTER *(Little Jane's dad)*: Jane?

(They quickly hide the wine and glasses.)

K.C.: Um, she can't come to the door right now, Mr. Baum-
garten. She's, uh, very upset.
WALTER: Tell her I want to talk to her. When she gets a chance.
K.C.: Well, I think that's not going to be for quite a long time,
actually, so, we'll, uh, come get you when and if she
feels like talking to you . . . You know, we tramps stick
together! *(Pause)* He's leaving. See?
LITTLE JANE: I can't believe you said that.
K.C.: He doesn't scare me.

BIG JANE: I can't believe you . . . said that . . .	K.C.: Yes, well, somebody had to. Now here's something:

LITTLE JANE: He's gone to get an ax.
K.C.: He won't remember. His brain is a puddle of phlegm.
LITTLE JANE: He knows we took the wine; he's going to break
down the door—
K.C.: Relax. He's *afraid* of you. Now listen:

LITTLE JANE: You are like . . . totally incredible! You are!	BIG JANE: You said that to him, you actually said that to him!

K.C. *(Overlapping)*: Yes, yes, I'm great, but: may I? Please?
Say something? Would that . . . ?
BIG JANE: What?
K.C.: I figured out that part of the song.
BIG JANE: Oh!
K.C.: Yes!

LITTLE JANE: Oh. Oh, great.	BIG JANE: You did!

K.C.: Yes, I had to listen to it about four hundred times. And my mother said, "Do we have to hear it one more time?"

LITTLE JANE: I still can't believe you said that to my father.

BIG JANE: Really.

K.C.: Let it go, Janes, it's just another one of the many high points of our life. Anyway, I pointed out to her that as much as I respected her as a woman and a wife and a mother, no one was interested in her musical opinion, so, SNAP OUT OF IT, YOU TWO! Okay . . . so . . . god, you got me all—*okay,* so from like *(She sings:)*

> I'm givin' it up—

LITTLE JANE: Right.

LITTLE JANE AND K.C.:
> Callin' it off,
> I don't wanna play—

K.C.:
> No, I don't wanna play—

LITTLE JANE:
> I'm lookin' ahead—

K.C.: No, wait—

LITTLE JANE: Oh.

K.C.:
> No, I don't wanna play—*hey!*

BIG JANE: Ohhhhhhh—

LITTLE JANE: Right.

K.C.: Yeah.

BIG JANE: It goes *down.*

K.C.: Yeah. So from—

BIG JANE: Is that my part?

K.C.: Right.

BIG JANE: Okay.

K.C. *(Spoken)*: And it's right
  on *(Sings:)*

	BIG JANE:
—I'm—lookin' a-*head*.	Right a-*head*.

K.C.: Right.
LITTLE JANE: Okay, so—
BIG JANE: *I* get it.
K.C.: Okay—
LITTLE JANE: I can't wait 'til we can do this!
BIG JANE: Really.
LITTLE JANE: We can go stand like in front of the bank at the
  mall!
BIG JANE: Right!
LITTLE JANE: The Three Tramps!
BIG JANE, LITTLE JANE AND K.C.: The Three Tramps! Yaaaay!
K.C. *(Spoken)*: Okay, from *(Sings:)*

  I'm givin' it up,

BIG JANE:
  Callin' it off,

LITTLE JANE:
  I don't wanna play.

BIG JANE AND K.C.:
  No, I don't wanna play—hey!

LITTLE JANE:	K.C. *(Spoken)*:
I'm lookin' ahead,	Right.
Fresh	BIG JANE *(Spoken)*:
Outa tears—	Right, okay.

K.C.: Okay, let's take it back from um—

BIG JANE: From—

K.C.: "Just see how the sun shines," okay— *(To Little Jane)*
        You can sing lead.

LITTLE JANE: Okay. And:

K.C.: And:

LITTLE JANE:
        Just see how the sun shines . . .

BIG JANE AND K.C.:
        Watch for the moon.

LITTLE JANE:
        Just see how the sun shines . . .

BIG JANE AND K.C.:
        Wish on the star.

K.C.: Whoo!

LITTLE JANE:
        Just see how the sun shines
        Without me.

BIG JANE: Okay.

K.C.:
        I'm givin' it up,

BIG JANE:
        Callin' it off,

LITTLE JANE:
        I don't wanna play.

BIG JANE AND K.C.:
        No, I don't wanna play—hey!

LITTLE JANE:

> I'm lookin' ahead,
> Fresh outa tears,
> Walkin' away.

BIG JANE AND K.C.:

> Yes, I'm a-walkin' away.

(They shriek.)

K.C.: Whoa!

BIG JANE: God!

LITTLE JANE: That is incredible!

BIG JANE: Isn't it?

K.C.: Isn't it?

LITTLE JANE: I *love* that song.

BIG JANE: Me, too.

BIG JANE AND K.C.: God.

BIG JANE: Let's go on.

LITTLE JANE *(To K.C.)*: What? . . .

(K.C. shakes her head.)

> What?

BIG JANE: Say it.

LITTLE JANE: Say it.

K.C.: I can't.

BIG JANE: We're not leaving here until you say—

LITTLE JANE: That's right.

BIG JANE: —what you were gonna say.

K.C.: You know what I feel like, though?

BIG JANE: What?

K.C.: . . . This is gonna sound queer.

LITTLE JANE: Say it!

BIG JANE: Say it.

K.C.: I feel like all the power . . . from this whole storm . . . is in us.

LITTLE JANE: I can't believe you said that.

K.C.: I do. I mean that.

BIG JANE: I know.

LITTLE JANE: I know just what you mean.

BIG JANE: I do, too.

K.C.: I feel like we *took* it or something.

BIG JANE: Yes.

K.C.: I feel like we could black out the whole *country* or something.

LITTLE JANE: Yes.

BIG JANE: Yes.

K.C.: If we wanted to?

LITTLE JANE: We could.

BIG JANE: To that.

K.C.: Yeah.

LITTLE JANE: Us.

(They clink their glasses; the lights and restaurant music restore to the present. The women resume their meal.)

K.C.: It's so . . . incredible.

LITTLE JANE: Isn't it?

BIG JANE *(Mimicking her)*: "Isn't it?" . . . It really is.

K.C.: *Montrachet?*

BIG JANE: You know all this *stuff.*

LITTLE JANE: Well, Bob's into Burgundy.

K.C.: An amusing little Burgundy.

BIG JANE: It's got legs.

K.C.: Yeesssss.

BIG JANE: And a nice nose.

LITTLE JANE: Oh, did you find a name for the dog? Speaking—you did? What?   K.C.: Uh-huh.

BIG JANE: Oh, what?

K.C.: Carl.

LITTLE JANE: Carl?

K.C.: Mm-hm.

LITTLE JANE: You called your Chinese wrinkle dog *Carl*?

BIG JANE: Carl?

K.C.: Mm-hm.

LITTLE JANE: Any particular reason?

K.C.: It was the girls' idea.

BIG JANE: I bet they miss their grandmom.

K.C.: That's not why we got the dog.

BIG JANE: No, I know.

K.C.: Then we would have just called the dog Nana and—

BIG JANE: No. That's not what I was saying! . . .

K.C.: I know.

BIG JANE: It's not!

LITTLE JANE: No, they know, kids know.

BIG JANE: Well, that's what I was saying.

LITTLE JANE: When something important happens. She was your mom and you're their mom . . .

K.C.: True. Maybe you should get Seth a puppy. Maybe that's what he's trying to tell you.

BIG JANE: That's it! He wants a dog!

K.C.: The mystery is solved! Is that awful?

LITTLE JANE: Please, if you think I haven't asked myself. Oh, the other night? . . . god . . . we had three of Bob's colleagues over, the boss, actually, and I didn't tell either of you this: Seth just charged into the living room like some madman with a mission and sank his teeth into this poor woman's thigh. What do you say? Oh, I'm so sorry, Mrs. Bluther, do you think you'll need stitches?

BIG JANE: Did she ask if she should get a rabies shot?

LITTLE JANE: No! But the funny, or not so funny, part was that Bob really was hoping to get a raise from her! And she was bleeding for about fifteen minutes! There was no way to pretend that our son hadn't bitten her with no provocation whatsoever. I guess it was just something about her . . .

BIG JANE: Karma.

(Walter stops to fill their wineglasses.)

LITTLE JANE: Hi, there. Oh, well, no raise.

BIG JANE: Really?

LITTLE JANE: No, he got it. It worked out. She was actually very nice about it. It just was . . .

(Walter's eyes lock with Little Jane's. He sings directly to her:)

WALTER:

I've been watching you for an hour.

LITTLE JANE *(Spoken, instantly serious)*: You have?

(Neither K.C. nor Big Jane responds to this.)

WALTER:

I've been thinking about your legs.

(Walter licks a drop of wine off the neck of the bottle, then sets it down, and moves away.)

K.C.: This isn't quite as bad, but I remember my mom complaining that my sister and I would say anything at all to *anybody* in public—

BIG JANE: I remember.

LITTLE JANE: Uh-huh.

K.C.: —and there was this local TV show, kids' show, in Cincinnati, this was right before we moved here, and—

(The sound of K.C.'s words drops out, her mouth moving silently through:)

WALTER:

I've been watching you use your fingers.

(Once again audible:)

K.C.: On the air, *live*. In front of God and everybody.

BIG JANE: Did they put you up for adoption?

(Again, the conversation fades out in time for Walter to sing:)

WALTER:
You do this thing when you grip your glass.

(Walter expresses an internalized "Mmm!" of pleasure as he walks away from the table and out of the room; Big Jane sees Little Jane watching him.)

BIG JANE *(Once again audible)*: What's the matter? You need something?
LITTLE JANE: I was wondering where the bathrooms are.
BIG JANE: You want me to ask?
LITTLE JANE: I can do it.

(Walter comes out of the kitchen with the two appetizers, and a very big pepper mill tucked under his arm.)

WALTER:
Oo, hoo, la la la, la la la, la la la.

(He sets the plates down.)

BIG JANE: God.

WALTER *(Directly to Little Jane)*:
I've been turning you over in my mind.

LITTLE JANE *(Nonchalant)*: Thanks. Not too much.

(Walter gives the pepper mill a few loving twists over Little Jane's mousse. K.C. waves; she wants pepper, too. He gives her one cursory little twist, then continues singing to Little Jane:)

WALTER:
Mm, hm, la la la, la la la, la la la—

LITTLE JANE: Thank you.   K.C.: Thanks.

(Walter moves away again.)

BIG JANE: You didn't ask.

LITTLE JANE: I know. I was looking at the size of that pepper
mill.

*(Walter suddenly moves in on Little Jane; during the fol-
lowing, she will leave her chair, and the two will move
throughout the restaurant as Big Jane and K.C. continue
talking, mouths moving silently. One or both of them will
occasionally address—as well as respond to—the empty
chair where Little Jane once sat.)*

WALTER:

Ho, it's not every night,
Not every night
That someone like you walks in the cafe.
Other women come in,
They don't begin
To stir me like you do.
By the way,
I've been thinking about your panties.
I've been guessing they might be pink.

BILL:

No no. Black.

WALTER:

And it's giving me shakes.
I've been making mistakes.

BILL:

Oh, the way you fit in that chair.

WALTER AND BILL:

Oo, hoo, la la la, la la la, la la la.

WALTER:

> I've been thinking of *you*, Jane, 'til it hurts.

WALTER AND BILL:

> Mmmm, oo, hoo, la la la, la la love.

BILL:

> The way you sit,

WALTER:

> The way you smile,

BILL:

> The way you talk,

WALTER AND BILL:

> The way you . . .
> The way you move me.
>
> Oh, it's not every night,
> Not every night
> That someone like you
> Walks in the cafe.
> And you're makin' me sweat,
> I'm gettin' wet,
> 'Cause women like you
> Come not every day.
> I've been havin' these thoughts
> I've never had.
> Boy, you've been giving me thoughts.
> I've been a bad boy.

K.C. *(Addresses Little Jane's empty chair)*: How's the mousse?
LITTLE JANE *(From across the room)*: Fabulous, you want a
bite? Take some. Take more, take it all.
BIG JANE *(Tasting K.C.'s soup)*: Mmmm.

LITTLE JANE:

> Mmmm.

WALTER AND BILL:
>Mmmm.

LITTLE JANE:
>La la la la la.

BIG JANE: God.

WALTER:	BILL:	LITTLE JANE:
God	Yes	*Finish it.* Please!
Oh	. . .	
God	Yes	
God	. . .	
Oh	Yes	
God		

WALTER AND BILL:
>Jane, Jane, Jane, Jane, Jane, Jane, Jane, Jane.

WALTER:
>I've been driving you down to Jersey.

BILL:
>I've been flying you off to London.

WALTER:
>I've been taking you to this cheap motel.

BILL:
>I've been touching you on the plane.

WALTER:
>Now you're treating me nice.

BILL:
>I'm under your skirt.

WALTER:
>I've been running for ice.

BILL:

> You're clutching my shirt.

WALTER:

> And I'm watching you.

BILL:

> You.

WALTER:

> I keep watching you.

BILL:

> 'Cause it's not every night,

WALTER AND BILL:

> Not every night
> Not every night
> There's someone like . . .
> Quite so hot every night,
> Not every night.
> Not every night
> There's someone like . . .

BILL:

> The way you sit,
> The way you smile,
> The way you talk,
> The way you . . .
> The way you smell,
> The way you laugh,
> The way you . . .
> The way you
>   walk in a room,
> The way you . . .
> The way you
>   move in that blouse,
> The way . . .

WALTER:

> The way you move
>   . . .
> The way you
>   walk in a room,
> The way you touch,
> The way you
>   butter your bread,
> The way you tease,
> The way . . .
> The way . . .

The way you
    dressed for me tonight.
	The way you
	    dressed for me tonight,
	J-J-J-Jane.

The way you . . .	The way you . . .
The way you . . .	The way you . . .
The way you . . .	The way you . . .
The way you . . .	The way you . . .
The way you . . .	The way you . . .
The way . . .	The way . . .
The way . . .	The way . . .
The way you . . .	The way you . . .
Make me your slave.	Cross your legs.
Make me your slave, Jane.	Sip your wine, Jane.
Make me your slave.	Wipe your mouth.
Make me your slave.	

WALTER:

    Not every night . . . not every . . .

WALTER AND BILL:

    The way you . . .
    The way you . . .
    The way you . . .
    The way you . . .
    The way you . . .
    The way you . . .
    The way you . . .
    The way you . . .

(The music fades out by the time Big Jane speaks; the women become five year olds, Walter their teacher.)

BIG JANE: Mr. Fuller! . . . Mr. Fuller!

WALTER: Yes, Jane?

BIG JANE: Um, can we make the tables into—

WALTER: We don't talk with our mouth full, Jane.

BIG JANE: I do!

WALTER: Finish chewing and then swallow what you're eating and then ask me your question.

K.C.: Mr. Fuller?

WALTER: Chew it well. Yes, K.C.?

K.C.: Is it . . . it must be uncomfortable having that mushroom hanging upside down from your bagina.

WALTER: Having—? What? No, that's not, that's a question for your mother and father, K.C. We don't talk like that in front of our friends. That's very important.

K.C.: Why?

WALTER: Because. We just don't.

BIG JANE: Can—? Mr. Fuller? *I finished chewing!*

WALTER: Okay, Jane. What?

BIG JANE: Can we make the tables and chairs into a hospital if we—*wait*—if we promise to put them all back when we're finished and stuff like that?

WALTER: Well . . . Why don't you ask K.C. if she would like to play? Since it's her first day.

BIG JANE: Okay.

WALTER: K.C.? Would you like to play a game with Jane and Jane? . . . You would?

K.C.: Everybody's named Jane.

WALTER: All right, everyone show K.C. how you play your game since she's the new one today.

BIG JANE: This'll be the hospital, okay?

LITTLE JANE: Okay, baby, here we go.

BIG JANE: Here we go.

K.C.: Here we go.

BIG JANE: Oh no! Oh no!

LITTLE JANE: What?

BIG JANE: The baby has no leg!

LITTLE JANE: Oh no.

K.C.: Oh no! Look!

BIG JANE: Where's the ambulance!?

LITTLE JANE: You have   K.C.: Look! HEY!
to call the operator!

(Big Jane makes the sound of a siren.)

LITTLE JANE: Wait, I haven't called yet!

K.C.: Look! You guys! It's hard to tell Barbie's bagina from her heinie. You see?

WALTER: K.C., what did I tell you? Those are things we don't discuss . . . Those are *private*.

LITTLE JANE: Here it comes, here comes the ambulance!

BIG JANE: Help, help, my leg's come off! We have to go to the hospital. *(To K.C)* You be the mommy.

K.C.: NO!

BIG JANE: Yes, we have to go.

K.C.: No, this, this is the special leg-fixing stick!

BIG JANE: Okay.

K.C.: This'll fix it up.

(Little Jane inaudibly lectures the Barbie doll during:)

BIG JANE: Okay, okay, let me have it!

K.C.: No!

BIG JANE: Yes, come on!

WALTER: Jane? You remember what we said about sharing?

(Big Jane thinks about this for a moment.)

BIG JANE: Okay, you can have the special stick.

WALTER: That's very good.

BIG JANE: And I have the special towel! *(She takes K.C.'s scarf)* Okay, here we go!

K.C.: No, let me have that!

BIG JANE: No! NO!

(They fight over the scarf; K.C. gets it back.)

WALTER: K.C., you have to share with Jane as well. Do you know what it means to share?

LITTLE JANE *(Suddenly an adult)*: NO! She doesn't! And she never will, either, I can assure you.

K.C. *(Also an adult)*: Oh come on, it was my scarf; he was a total fascist.

LITTLE JANE: I'm not talking about the scarf.

K.C.: What is it you want me to share, Jane, my happiness?

BIG JANE *(Also an adult)*: Hey, hey—!

K.C.: I'm sorry you're unhappy, I can't do anything about that.

BIG JANE: We're not the enemy, remember? We're in each other's corner.

WALTER: Sharing means you've had a proper upbringing. It's just one of the ways we can tell when a little girl has had the correct—

BIG JANE: Oh, fuck you!

(They all return to their childhood scene.)

WALTER: Show them you know what it means to share, K.C., and let Jane have the scarf for a little while and then you can have it back and you can both take turns. Back and forth.

(K.C. does not relinquish the scarf.)

All right, then let me have the scarf.

(He holds out his hand. She does not give him the scarf.)

K.C.? All right, then you have to go back to your seat if you can't share. And everyone will have to sit quietly for a moment while K.C. thinks about sharing. I'm very sorry.

(Big Jane, Little Jane and K.C. silently obey.)

Maybe when K.C. feels like sharing, we can all go back to our game, but not before.

K.C.: Can . . . ?

WALTER: Yes?

K.C.: Where is the telephone, please?

WALTER: Why? You need to make a phone call?

K.C.: Yes, please.

WALTER: You do? No, you can't call your mother, K.C. You'll have to wait until you get home.

K.C.: I told her I would call, I promised . . .

WALTER: No, you didn't.

K.C. *(Becoming hysterical)*: Yes! She said I should call from school! I have to call. I told her I would call! I did!

WALTER: No, it's all right, all right, all right, K.C., we'll see about calling your mother.

K.C.: *I* HAVE TO DO IT!

WALTER: All right, don't cry now. Class, I'm going to take K.C . . . .No . . . K.C., do you know where the phone is? I can't leave everyone alone. You remember the principal's office? All right, when you go—right outside the door—you walk all the way down—

(As he points the way, the lights in the restaurant return to normal and the restaurant music pops back in; all three women are looking up at Walter.)

Behind the bar and to your right. The double doors.

LITTLE JANE: Thank you.

WALTER: Finished?

LITTLE JANE: Thank you.

(Walter collects their appetizer plates.)

BIG JANE: It was wonderful, both of them. I tried them.

(Walter moves off.)

LITTLE JANE: So anyway, the whole upshot is I got two new clients all of a sudden.

K.C.: You're kidding.

BIG JANE: Congratulations. What?

LITTLE JANE: Well, a fabric softener and a cookie, and they're both actually sort of interesting, as far as . . . The fabric softener has no harmful chemicals in it—

BIG JANE: Great.

LITTLE JANE: —and the cookie uses natural sweeteners, so I'm obviously becoming the Green Spokesperson at . . . work . . . which is—

(Bill begins banging on the piano.)

(To Bill) Honey? That's very distracting, please, Mommy can't think if you do that.

(He stops.)

(To the women) I mean, they may not be the most lucrative campaigns either, but at the same time I don't have to lose sleep—

BIG JANE: Exactly.

LITTLE JANE: —over the horrible things I'm doing to little children, causing cancer—

(Bill begins banging on the keys again.)

(To Bill) Seth, I asked you to play softly, now I mean it! I'm going to take away all your Transformers and your Sega Genesis and Power Rangers, and I'm going to put them all in a pile outside the house and burn them, and you'll never see them again. All right? It's up to you. It's your choice.

(The banging does not stop.)

(To the women) Excuse me. *(She stands, moves to the piano)* Why are you doing this? We love you. Daddy and I love you very much. Why are you acting this way? Why are you *biting people, can't you tell me?* . . .

(She exits. Bill resumes playing restaurant music. At the table, K.C. is now holding an invisible infant.)

BIG JANE: Oh my god . . . Oh my god!

K.C.: Isn't she great?

BIG JANE: She's alive.

K.C.: That, too.

BIG JANE: She's real.

K.C.: I know, I keep thinking, Who is this person?

BIG JANE: Marsha?

K.C.: We think. Do you like it?

BIG JANE: Oh yeah! *(To baby)* Look at you! Oh. She's so beautiful.

K.C.: You think?

BIG JANE: Oh, are you serious? *(To baby)* Look! You have fingernails! Hi, there. You have perfect, look how perfect they are.

K.C.: Uh-huh.

BIG JANE: Can she see?

K.C.: Uh-huh.

BIG JANE: She can? She can see us?

K.C.: They can see in the womb.

BIG JANE: Really? A womb with a view!

K.C.: You go outside, they see a red glow.

BIG JANE: Oh, I hope someday I'll have something to be proud of. I mean, oh—

K.C.: What do you mean?

BIG JANE: I don't know what I mean. It isn't—

K.C.: You can have babies.

BIG JANE: No, I know, it isn't, I wouldn't take anything away from what you—

K.C.: I know.

BIG JANE *(Continuous)*: —and Jane have, and it isn't, I know you know, but . . .

K.C.: I understand.

BIG JANE: It wouldn't any of it be right for me, I just . . . Ohhhhhh . . .

(Walter arrives with the entrées.)

WALTER: The duck?

211

K.C.: Here. And the veal over there.

(Big Jane looks up into Walter's face as he serves her.)

BIG JANE: Hi, my name is Jane Ingham and I'm calling from
   Publisher's Clearing House? We're offering an incredible . . .

WALTER: *Bon appétit.*

BIG JANE: *Bon appétit!*

(He moves away.)

K.C.: You just wished him a good appetite.

BIG JANE: I know. But he might be hungry, too, right?

*(Little Jane returns from the bathroom. She addresses
Walter; both stand.)*

LITTLE JANE: Hi.

WALTER: Hi.

LITTLE JANE: What's wrong? . . . Did something happen?

WALTER: No, nothing happened, I wish it had. Where's Seth?

LITTLE JANE: He's gone to bed. Are you all right?

WALTER: No, I'm not.

LITTLE JANE: What?

WALTER: I'm not all right.

LITTLE JANE: Tell me.

WALTER: I'm sorry I'm so late. I know you wanted to celebrate: happy birthday to me.

LITTLE JANE: It's okay.

WALTER: It seems . . . to me we've tried everything, gone
   around every bush, jumped through every hoop . . . to
   try and . . . Couples therapy, family therapy, individual
   therapy, it's a fucking orgy of psychiatrists around here
   and . . . I don't think that's . . . I think it's you. Jane.

LITTLE JANE: You're drunk. Aren't you—?

WALTER: So what I feel doesn't mean anything, is that it?

LITTLE JANE: No.

WALTER: Just the way you're doing that right now. Everything about you, Jane. The way you sit, the way you smile, the way you talk, the way you smell, all the things I'm supposed to love about you: the way you laugh, the way you walk in a room, the way you dressed for me tonight and put on this music . . . I have never liked this song. Why do you insist on thinking this song has some sentimental value for me? The way you butter your bread, sip your wine . . . You know what it is? I swear I've figured it out: you're little. Honest to god. You're "Little Jane." You have to control everything: "Quick, go make him coffee," I can see your mind clicking away furiously to try and fix it, you can't! You can't fix it. "Turn off the music, he doesn't like it." What is it that is so wrong with me that you have to fiddle and fuck with it? Can't I be this? Can't I be . . . ?

LITTLE JANE: Yes.

WALTER: You can't have it all your way, and no matter how much you read and think you know, be the first on your block to know everything about abso-fucking-lutely every subject under the sun, you're still . . . You'll always be . . . you. And . . . I'm sorry . . . I have come . . . to hate it . . . I hate you. *(Short pause)* But life goes on. Right? . . .

(Walter moves off. Bill speaks, answering a phone.)

BILL: Hello?

BIG JANE: Hi, my name is Jane Ingham and—

BILL: Who?

BIG JANE: Oh, you don't know me, but let me ask you a question: do you read magazines?

BILL: No.

BIG JANE: No? Why?

BILL: I'm blind.

BIG JANE: . . . Oh.

WALTER *(Starts a new call)*: Hello?

BIG JANE: Hi, I'm calling from Publisher's Clearing House. We're offering a special—

WALTER: Are you the people with that *fucking*: "Think about your daydreams"? Fuck you. Eat shit and die! Ten million dollars my butt!

LITTLE JANE *(Suddenly a toddler)*: 'Lo?

BIG JANE: Hi, my name is Jane Ingham.

LITTLE JANE: Dnlanla?

BIG JANE: What?

LITTLE JANE: Aaaaaa . . .

BIG JANE: Oh, darling, put your mother on . . . Could I . . . Let me talk to your mommy please? . . . Never mind . . . . . . Bye bye!

K.C. *(To an invisible child)*: Who is it? Is it Nana? . . . . . . Let me have the phone. . . . *Now.*

(Big Jane hangs up; K.C. speaks into the phone:)

K.C.: What do chicken pox look like? . . . They do? . . . Shit. No, listen, I'm gonna go freak out . . . No, I'll call you later. I'll—I don't know when, bye. Bye. Mom! *(She hangs up)*

BILL: Hello?

BIG JANE: Hi, please don't hang up, please please, I'm being held prisoner by these people, I don't know who they are, I swear, I don't even know where they're keeping me, all I know is they've agreed to let me go on one condition and that's that you take a year's subscription to one of their magazines . . . Hello?

WALTER *(Starting new phone call)*: Hello?

BIG JANE: Hi, my name is Jane Ingham and I'm going to lose my job if somebody doesn't subscribe to one of these stupid magazines, so I'll pay for the subscription, all right?—whatever—hello?

LITTLE JANE *(Starting another call)*: Hello?

BIG JANE: Hi, my name is Jane Ingham and you *do* know me.

LITTLE JANE: Hi, what's up?

BIG JANE: Well, seriously, I thought maybe I'd try some of my new selling techniques on someone I knew first, all right? . . . So just bear with me and obviously you don't have to buy anything, okay . . .

(Little Jane turns away.)

Jane? . . . It's not funny, come on . . .

(K.C. goes into labor; Walter rushes to her side.)

WALTER: Is this it? Okay, keep breathing.

K.C.: Call my mom.

WALTER: I will.

K.C.: No, now! NOW!

WALTER *(Running off)*: Okay.

BILL *(Yet another new phone call)*: Yello?

BIG JANE: Hi, my name is Jane Ingham and I want to ask you something: do you read magazines?

BILL: Uh-huh.

BIG JANE: You do?

BILL: Uh-huh.

BIG JANE: How refreshing. God. Okay, great, let's see . . .

BILL: Can I ask you something?

BIG JANE: Sure.

BILL: What are you wearing?

BIG JANE *(Leaves the table. Sings)*:
  I'm givin' it up,

K.C. *(Sings)*:
  Callin' it off,

LITTLE JANE *(Sings)*:
  I don't wanna play.

BIG JANE AND K.C. *(Sing)*:
No, I don't wanna play,   LITTLE JANE *(Sings)*:
hey!   I'm lookin' ahead.
                                            Fresh outa tears!
                                            Walkin' away!

BIG JANE, LITTLE JANE AND K.C. *(Sing)*:
Yes, I'm a-walkin' away!

(They shriek, as before.)

K.C.: Whoa!
BIG JANE: God!
LITTLE JANE: That is incredible.
BIG JANE: Isn't it?
K.C.: Isn't it?
LITTLE JANE: I *love* that song.
BIG JANE: Me, too.
BIG JANE AND K.C.: God.
LITTLE JANE: What? Say it!
BIG JANE: Say it! *(Beat)* Have you talked to Case?
LITTLE JANE: No. Have you?
K.C.: Have you talked to Jane?
BIG JANE: No.
LITTLE JANE: Have you talked to Jane?
K.C.: No. Have you?
BIG JANE *(Overlapping "have you?")*: Have you talked to Jane?
LITTLE JANE *(Overlapping "Jane?")*: Jane? No, why? Have
you?
K.C.: Have you—?
LITTLE JANE: Have you talked to—
BIG JANE: No. Why?
K.C.: Have you heard from Jane?
LITTLE JANE: Have you?
K.C.: No. Have you?

(Pause. They sing:)

BIG JANE:

> Jane,
> You would love this hotel.
> My flight was okay.
> Boy, that water's blue.
> I go snorkeling today.
> The suit fits me fine.
> See you Wednesday night.
> Pass this on to K.C.,
> Jane.

BIG JANE:

> Jane,
> Thank you, thank you,
>   thank you.
> This vacation was the
>   greatest idea.
> I met this guy,
> He teaches snorkeling.
> I won't be home 'til
>   Thursday,
> Or at the latest Friday.
> I found that perfume you
>   asked for.
> Give you a call the minute
>   I get in.
> Pass it on to K.C.,
> Jane.

LITTLE JANE:

> Jane,
> You would love this
>   hotel.
> My flight was okay.
> Boy, that water's blue.
> I go snorkeling today.
> The suit fits me fine.
> See you Wednesday night.
>   Pass this on to K.C.,
> Jane.

BIG JANE:

> Jane,
> Have left my
>   hotel,
> And moved in
>   with Philippe.
> I'm gonna stay
>   down here
>   awhile.

LITTLE JANE:

> Jane,
> Thank you,
>   thank you,
>   thank you.
> This vacation
>   was the
>   greatest idea.
> I met this guy,

K.C.:

> Jane,
> You would love
>   this hotel.
> My flight was
>   okay.
> Boy, that water's
>   blue.
> I go snorkeling

You know me.
Please call my
    mother
And tell her I'm
    fine.
Philippe says
    hello.
Pass this on to
    K.C.
Yo ho ho, and a
    bottle of rum.
Your island girl.

He teaches
    snorkeling.
I won't be home
    'til Thursday,
Or at the latest
    Friday.
I found that
    perfume you
    asked for.
Give you a call
    the minute I
    get in.
Pass it on to K.C.,
Jane.

today.
The suit fits me
    fine.
See you Wed-
    nesday night.
Pass this on to
    K.C.,
Jane.

LITTLE JANE:

Jane,
Have left my hotel,
And moved in with Philippe.
I'm gonna stay down here
    awhile.
You know me.
Please call my mother
And tell her I'm fine.
Philippe says hello.
Pass this on to K.C.
Yo ho ho,
And a bottle of rum.
Your island girl.

K.C.:

Jane,
Thank you, thank you,
    thank you.
This vacation was the
    greatest idea.
I met this guy,
He teaches snorkeling.
I won't be home 'til
    Thursday,
Or at the latest Friday.
I found that perfume you
    asked for.
Give you a call the minute
    I get in.
Pass it on to K.C.,
Jane.

K.C.:

Jane,
Have left my hotel,
And moved in with Philippe.

I'm gonna stay down here awhile.
You know me.
Please call my mother
And tell her I'm fine.
Philippe says hello.
Pass this on to K.C.
Yo ho ho, and a bottle of rum.
Your island girl,

BIG JANE, LITTLE JANE AND K.C.:
    Jane.

(The women return to the table; restaurant music restores. The women start talking; they are mid-discussion.)

BIG JANE: But didn't Congress like consider actually backing the Nazis for awhile?

LITTLE JANE: Yes. Yes!

K.C.: I don't believe that.

LITTLE JANE: No, it's true. *(To Big Jane)* Try the veal.

K.C.: I don't believe it.

LITTLE JANE: Well, okay, I don't believe the world is round either. What does that—?

K.C.: I think it was simply a question of pleasing their constituents, as always, and they didn't want to offend those that were German.

LITTLE JANE: Oh, come on.

K.C.: They certainly didn't know he was going to kill six million Jews.

BIG JANE: Mmmmm!   LITTLE JANE: No one knew.

K.C.: But you're saying—

LITTLE JANE: I'm saying that Joseph Kennedy wanted the Communists out of Germany and Howard Hughes—

K.C. *(Dismissive)*: Ohhhh.

LITTLE JANE: Howard Hughes wanted to sell munitions—

BIG JANE: I believe that.

LITTLE JANE: —and J. Paul Getty knew he'd make more money—

K.C.: Congress does not . . .

LITTLE JANE: What?

K.C.: You're making it sound like our own leaders are so totally cynical—

LITTLE JANE: They are!

K.C.: Well . . . not like that. Agreed, they're pigs, but not—

LITTLE JANE: Look at what's happening right now.

K.C.: Stalin, I don't care *what you say,* Stalin and any totalitarian government is worse than anything the United States Congress can cook up.

LITTLE JANE: So?

K.C.: What do you mean, "So?"

LITTLE JANE: I don't mean, "So?," but what's your point?

K.C.: My point is you make it sound like bad us, we should have known in advance.

LITTLE JANE: We did! *Mein Kampf* had been published, it wasn't a secret what this guy had in mind.

K.C.: You just said, "No one knew." Look, the Nazis were stopped because of us, and Stalin meanwhile formed a non-aggression pact with Hitler—

LITTLE JANE: I know all this—

K.C.: —and—I mean, *GOD!* My mother used to do the same thing, and it drove me crazy then and it drives me crazy now. You present your opinion as if it's fact and it's not a fact. Jane.

LITTLE JANE: What's not a fact?

K.C.: Your analysis.

LITTLE JANE *(Small pause; evenly)*: Okay.

K.C.: I mean . . .

BIG JANE: Urinalysis?

K.C.: . . . She would read some stupid article in *Life* magazine, suggesting that the pill *might* cause cancer, and then from there we would make a qualitative leap to it does cause cancer, and you do the same thing. Your way of seeing things is the only truth . . . You're very insistent, and you're very persuasive, but sometimes I just feel railroaded by you.

(Short pause.)

LITTLE JANE: I'm sorry.

K.C.: No . . . I feel like, all night, the two of you have been trying to get me to *cry*. I don't want to cry. I don't feel like crying. My way isn't the same as yours.

LITTLE JANE: I know. I respect that.

K.C.: No . . . I feel like . . .

LITTLE JANE: Bob says I do the same thing.

K.C.: Well, he's wrong, and I'm right. No, but you know, I mean . . . I don't *want* to get angry at her. I don't feel angry at her.

LITTLE JANE: Who said you had to get angry?

(Small pause.)

K.C.: Maybe I do.

LITTLE JANE: It's okay. Whatever.

(Pause.)

BIG JANE *(Referring to wine)*: Are we allowed to pour this?

LITTLE JANE: No, Jane, the wine police will come and then you die.

K.C.: I'm sorry.

LITTLE JANE: Don't apologize.

K.C.: . . . I keep thinking about her when she was my age.

LITTLE JANE: Uh-huh.

K.C.: Or even younger.

(Pause. K.C. is about to speak, stops.)

LITTLE JANE: What?

(K.C. shakes her head. The two women are looking at her.)

K.C. *(Sings)*:

> In her hand she holds a small bouquet.
> In the distance there's a Chevrolet.
> In the corner there's a tree
> Only half of which we see
> In the churchyard with the bride
> And the soldier at her side.
>
> And she's got wavy hair.
> And she wears her shoulders all but bare.
> And the soldier looks her way
> On a breezy Brooklyn day
> In the forties
> In the fall
> In the picture
> In the hall.
>
> And a cloud is passing by
> In the movement of the sky.
> And it's captured like the faces
> And the flowers
> And the car
> And the gown
> In a hundred shades of brown
> In the churchyard
> In the fall
> In the picture
> In the hall.
>
> On the wall—
>   feelings whirling 'round and around.
> In the hall—
>   gravel on the ground.
> I recall—
> Listening for the sound without sound,
> 'Round and around.
>
> There's a frame around the breezy day.
> There's a path around the tree.

There's an arm around the bride,
And a private sort of pride
In the woman
In the fall
In the silence
In the hall
In the rustling
In the gown
In the hundred shades of brown
In the churchyard
In the breeze
In the whirling
In the freeze
In the feeling
In the fall
In the picture
In the hall,

Frozen in the fall
In the forties
On the wall.

(Restaurant music resumes. K.C. looks at the two women.)

BIG JANE: We understand.
K.C.: Anybody want some of this?

(Walter arrives beside them.)

WALTER: How is everything?
LITTLE JANE: Fine. Thanks.

(He fills their water glasses. As before, Walter's eyes connect with Little Jane's.)

WALTER: You can't fix it. You can't have it all your way, and no matter how much you read and think you know, be the first one on your block to know everything about abso-fucking-lutely—

LITTLE JANE: Wait. That's . . . really terribly, terribly interesting, honey, but . . . may I say something? *(She sings a cappella to Walter, soon joined by the piano:)*

> You think that the sun will shine
> The way it did before.
> You think that those moonlit nights
> Will still be at the shore.
> You think that our lucky star
> Is yours forever more.

> Well, just see how the sun shines . . .

(K.C. and Big Jane sing backup:)

BIG JANE AND K.C.:
> Just watch for the moon.

LITTLE JANE:
> Just see how the sun shines . . .

BIG JANE AND K.C.:
> Just wish on that star.

LITTLE JANE:
> Just see how the sun shines
> Without me.

BIG JANE AND K.C.:
> You're gonna be sorry.

(Walter disappears. The three women perform full-front.)

LITTLE JANE:
> I saw you with Marianne.
> Imagine my surprise.
> You told me that you were mine.
> Imagine all the lies.

Now darlin' imagine me
With lots of other guys.

And, just see how the sun shines . . .

BIG JANE AND K.C.:
Just watch for the moon.

LITTLE JANE:
Just see how the sun shines . . .

BIG JANE AND K.C.:
Just wish on the star.

LITTLE JANE:
Just see how the sun shines
Without me.

K.C.:
I'm givin' it up,

BIG JANE:
Callin' it off,

LITTLE JANE:
I don't wanna play.

BIG JANE AND K.C.:
No, I don't wanna play—hey!

LITTLE JANE:
I'm lookin' ahead,
Fresh outa tears,
Walkin' away.

BIG JANE AND K.C.
Yes, I'm a-walkin' away.

LITTLE JANE:

> And I know someday
> You're gonna feel the pain.
> Baby, before you know
> You'll hear a sad refrain.
> You'll think how it used to be,
> And through the pouring rain
>
> You'll see how the sun shines . . .

BIG JANE AND K.C.:

> It ain't gonna shine.

LITTLE JANE:

> Just see how it shines
> Without me.

> *(Music continues; Little Jane speaks:)*

> Look at my eyes,
> My eyes are dry.
> Look at my lips,
> They're saying good-bye.
> Look at the sky,
> It's turning gray.
> And take a look at this:

> *(Points to her butt and sings:)*

> It's walkin' away!

BIG JANE AND K.C.:

> I'm through with talkin'
> I'm a-walkin'
> Just a-walkin' away!

LITTLE JANE:

> And I know someday
> You're gonna feel the pain.

> Baby, before you know
> You'll hear a sad refrain.
> You'll think how it used to be,
> And through the pouring rain
> You'll see how the sun shines . . .

BIG JANE AND K.C.:
> It ain't gonna shine.

LITTLE JANE:
> Good luck with the moonlight . . .

BIG JANE AND K.C.:
> It ain't gonna shine.

LITTLE JANE:
> Just see how the sun shines
> Without me hangin' around.
> Just see how it shines
> Without me.

BIG JANE AND K.C.:
> Bye-bye. Bye. Bye-bye.

LITTLE JANE:
> Without me.

BIG JANE AND K.C.:
> Bye-bye. Bye. Bye-bye.

LITTLE JANE:
> Without me.

BIG JANE AND K.C.:
> Bye-bye. Bye. Bye-bye.

BIG JANE, LITTLE JANE AND K.C.:
> Without me!

(They collapse in their chairs, exhausted, laughing. Bill takes a break, leaves the stage. Big Jane pours the last of the wine.)

LITTLE JANE: Oh god!
BIG JANE: Aaaaaaa!

(Walter is at their side again.)

K.C.: Hello.
WALTER *(To Big Jane)*: Would you like me to take that?
BIG JANE: Oh, I'm sorry. They said I could pour it. Sorry.
WALTER: All finished?
K.C.: Yes.
LITTLE JANE: Thanks, it was great.
BIG JANE: Our eyes were bigger than our stomachs.
WALTER: Would you like some coffee or dessert?
K.C.: Just coffee.
LITTLE JANE: You sure? *(To Walter)* I'd like to see a dessert menu.
WALTER: I can tell you.
LITTLE JANE: Great.
BIG JANE: Oh boy! Here we go again.
WALTER: We have . . . fresh sorbets made on the premises. Strawberry and lime.
BIG JANE *(Cracking up again)*: No, I love lime.
WALTER: We also have a light butter sponge cake, an almond hazelnut torte.
BIG JANE: Mmmm.

(All three of the women lose it.)

LITTLE JANE: We just can't seem to have a good time.
BIG JANE: No!
K.C.: We can't.
WALTER: Our chocolate sin pie which has a layer of—
LITTLE JANE: I don't want to know.
WALTER: Okay.

LITTLE JANE: Yes, I do, yes I do!

WALTER: All right. Somebody should hose you three down. It has a layer of . . . It has, you see, you got me all confused, it has a chocolate graham-cracker crust, a layer of dark chocolate mousse, a thin layer of white chocolate cream, then a layer of bittersweet chocolate and whipped cream with Sambucca over the top.

(Bill reenters and resumes playing.)

BIG JANE: God.

K.C.: Not too rich.

WALTER: Mm-mm. We have a kumquat citrus tart, and rum-flavored apple aspic. Which is very good.

LITTLE JANE: I'll have that.

WALTER: And fresh peaches with cream.

LITTLE JANE: I'll have the aspic.

WALTER: Anyone else?

K.C.: Just coffee.

LITTLE JANE: And a cup of coffee.

(Walter moves off, taking their plates.)

K.C.: Oh well . . . *(Small pause)* I've actually got to get back.

BIG JANE: Ohhhhh.

K.C.: No, the baby-sitter looks a little . . .

BIG JANE: You're kidding.

K.C.: No, you *know?*, she *doesn't.* She just isn't my mom.

BIG JANE: Uh-huh.

K.C.: This is the first night, I think this is probably the first time . . . we've had to hire a sitter.

LITTLE JANE: Uh-huh.

K.C.: Is that possible? She died so suddenly . . . And she was always available . . . I just feel so weird about leaving them with a stranger.

BIG JANE: They'll be fine.

K.C.: I know. And it's really wonderful seeing you both.

BIG JANE: You, too.

(Little Jane kisses K.C.'s cheek.)

Yay!

(Walter arrives with coffee.)

He's wonderful, your piano player.

WALTER: Mittens? Yeah, he's okay. *(To Little Jane)* I'll have your dessert in a second. *(He moves away once more)*

BIG JANE: Did he say *he* was gonna have your dessert?

(Pause.)

LITTLE JANE: You know what it was about the particles?

K.C.: Particles?

LITTLE JANE: I was telling Jane how I'd had this experience as a kid where I'm standing in this room?

BIG JANE: Mm-hm?

LITTLE JANE: And . . . I've always remembered this, because I'm not doing anything, I'm just standing there . . . And . . . I don't know, I have this feeling which I can never describe, it's like it changes or something.

K.C.: Uh-huh?

LITTLE JANE: But it's very profound . . . and I feel if I could just . . .

(Pause.)

K.C.: Say it.

LITTLE JANE: Yes.

K.C.: Find the right words—

LITTLE JANE: Yes.

K.C.: —for whatever it is. Because you don't want to sully it with clichés.

LITTLE JANE: *Yes.*

K.C.: With what you're "supposed" to say.

LITTLE JANE: That's exactly it. God. *(Pause)* And . . . then there was this thing in the paper about these subatomic particles actually changing what they do when the scientists starting watching them.

BIG JANE: Uh-huh.

LITTLE JANE: And I thought: wouldn't it be incredible . . .

(Pause.)

K.C.: *Yes.*

LITTLE JANE: . . . if all the secrets of the universe were aware when we started to get close to them?

K.C.: Yes.

LITTLE JANE: And they changed.

K.C.: Exactly.

BIG JANE: . . . *Oh!*

LITTLE JANE: Or did something sneaky.

K.C.: *Uh-huh!*

LITTLE JANE: Because they didn't want us to know!

K.C.: Well, they were *secrets.*

LITTLE JANE: Right.

BIG JANE: Exactly.

(Pause.)

K.C.: Fucking particles.

(Walter arrives with the aspic.)

WALTER: There you go.

LITTLE JANE: Thank you.

(He produces three forks and places them beside the aspic.)

WALTER: That's in case you decide to *share.*

LITTLE JANE: What, are you kidding?

BIG JANE: Mmmmmm.

LITTLE JANE: Keep your greedy fingers out of there!

BIG JANE AND K.C.: Ohhhh, please? *Please?*

LITTLE JANE: Get out, get out! *(To Walter)* Oh, I'll take the check, whenever you get a second.

(Walter exits. Bill sings:)

BILL:

We never notice 'til it's gone.
Notice how a minute flies,
    the second hand is on the two
A year can flash before your eyes.
That's a trick a year can do.
On and on, we sweep the four.
Now you see it, now you don't.
That's the way a season dies,
    vanishing in open air.
But now you're wond'ring where we are,
More than halfway there.
We pass the seven and approach the eight now,
On and on we climb
And never seem to see it go
'Til it's almost time.
It's almost time.
Time.

(The women are now in their late seventies.)

K.C.: How's Bob?
BIG JANE: Don't you two have a big anniversary coming up?
LITTLE JANE: We had it.
K.C.: Fifty?
LITTLE JANE: Fifty years.
K.C.: You're a better man than I, Gunga Din.
BIG JANE: Did he know it was his anniversary?

(Little Jane shakes her head no.)

K.C.: Does he still go in and out?
LITTLE JANE: Some. Not as much.
BIG JANE: Go in and out?
LITTLE JANE: Of his thoughts.
BIG JANE: Oh. I thought you meant of the *house*!

LITTLE JANE: That he does. Drives the nurse insane.
     I have to keep saying, Let her handle it. He knows
     in the garden, so . . . I used to think if he quit drinking,
     everything would be easier. I got my way. Then
     I thought, Once Seth finishes medical school and gets
     established . . . Then I thought, Once Bob retires.

BIG JANE: It never is.

LITTLE JANE: And the reward for all the struggle is always
     something harder than the thing before. That's why
     I love plants. They go where you put 'em, they don't talk
     back, they're beautiful. If they die, you buy another one.

BIG JANE: I think you're handling it beautifully. *(Pause)* You are.

(K.C. affectionately tucks Little Jane's hair behind her ear.)

LITTLE JANE: I don't like my ears to show. No, they're too small.

K.C.: Oh yes, hide them.

LITTLE JANE: All right.

BIG JANE: Well . . . I have an announcement to make. *(Short
     pause)* I'm thinking of retiring.

K.C.: Oh, come on.

BIG JANE: I am. I haven't taken another patient for the last
     three years, and the last one is healthy, well, no, she's
     nuts, she doesn't need me, but she doesn't need me to
     tell her she doesn't need me, and I could go on listen-
     ing to her fantasies for another ten years or so, but . . .
     I'm gonna take some of the money I've saved up and
     travel for awhile.

LITTLE JANE: Where?

BIG JANE: I don't know,   K.C.: Wonderful . . .
I haven't—

BIG JANE *(To K.C.)*: Thank you. *(To Little Jane)* I haven't
     decided, where should I go?

BILL *(Sings)*:
          Rain, rain,
          City rain . . .

K.C.: Congratulations.

LITTLE JANE: That's great.

BIG JANE: Any ideas?

K.C.: Greece? Africa?

BILL:

> Rain, rain,
> New York rain . . .

LITTLE JANE: I wish I could leave Bob alone long enough to go with you.

BIG JANE: Come! Come with me!

K.C.: He wouldn't know you were gone, leave him with a . . .

LITTLE JANE: Stuffed dummy.

K.C.: Really!

LITTLE JANE: With my face painted on it . . . I'm a horrible human being.

(Small pause.)

BIG JANE: Think about it.

LITTLE JANE: I came in the room the other day and he was sitting with a little pad and a pencil, writing his name over and over. Trying to get the spelling. Robert with two "b"s. Kissel with a "c."

(Pause.)

K.C.: He doesn't want to lose . . .

LITTLE JANE: Himself.

BIG JANE: It's his name.

(Pause.)

K.C.: I remember my father saying that, "Somebody had better go through all these boxes of photographs and figure out who all these people were before nobody remembers." *(Short pause)* Who they were.

(Pause.)

LITTLE JANE: Oh, oh, did I tell you this? I told Nancy Latchaw
that Bob was incontinent now?

K.C.: You did tell me this.

BIG JANE: Listen anyway.

LITTLE JANE: And she said, "Oh, I thought you told me he
was at home with you."

*(Lights change, and they are once again in their thirties.
Walter arrives with the check, a pen and Little Jane's credit
card slip.)*

Thank you.

WALTER: More coffee?

LITTLE JANE: No, thank you.

BIG JANE: This was nice.

WALTER: I'm glad you enjoyed it. Come again.

BIG JANE: We will.

K.C.: We will.

WALTER: I'll have your coats up front, whenever you're ready.

(He moves away. Little Jane is filling out the slip.)

BIG JANE: Double the tax.

LITTLE JANE: Thank you, Jane.

K.C.: When do you start the job?

BIG JANE: Oh, anytime . . . but, we'll see.

LITTLE JANE: Did it rain?

(They begin gathering their things.)

K.C.: Oh, I don't know.

BIG JANE: I've got to get a cab.

LITTLE JANE: That makes two of us . . .

BIG JANE: You get your scarf?

K.C.: Oh, thank you.

LITTLE JANE: Say hi to Leo for me.

K.C.: I will.
BIG JANE: And Bob.
LITTLE JANE: I will.

(They are standing.)

BIG JANE: And listen, I'm a wonderful baby-sitter.
K.C.: Oh, I know. Thank you. I'll take you up on it.
BIG JANE: Good . . .
K.C.: How does anybody ever know who they are without their friends?
BIG JANE: Really.
K.C.: To blame.

(Pause. All five characters are looking front. They sing:)

ALL:

> I'm standing in this room,
> And I'm not doing anything,
> And I'm not moving,
> And I don't know . . .
> I just have this feeling
> I can't describe.

LITTLE JANE: I love the glass, don't you?
K.C.: Me, too. *(To Walter)* Thank you.
WALTER: G'night.
BIG JANE: 'Bye.
LITTLE JANE: Thanks again.

(As they begin to exit:)

> Oh, it did rain, I think.
K.C.: It's still coming down.
BIG JANE: There goes a cab, too.

(Walter begins clearing the table.)

LITTLE JANE: That's right, the last cab that will ever go by.
K.C.: There's another one.
BIG JANE: That's the last one.
LITTLE JANE: *That's* the last one.

(Walter blows out the candle from their table.)

END OF PLAY

CRAIG LUCAS's other plays include *Reckless, Blue Window, God's Heart, The Dying Gaul, The Singing Forest, Stranger* and *This Thing of Darkness* (with David Schulner). His screenplays include *Longtime Companion, Prelude to a Kiss, Reckless, Blue Window* (all directed by Norman René) and *The Secret Lives of Dentists* (directed by Alan Rudolph, starring Campbell Scott, Hope Davis and Denis Leary). With Mr. René he also created the musical, *Marry Me a Little,* with songs by Stephen Sondheim. He has recently completed the book for *The Light in the Piazza,* based on the novella by Elizabeth Spencer, with music and lyrics by Adam Guettel.

Mr. Lucas received the Excellence in Literature Award from the American Academy of Arts and Letters, the first George and Elisabeth Marton Award and the L.A. Drama Critics Award (all for *Blue Window*); the Drama-Logue and Burns Mantle Best Musical awards (for *Three Postcards*); two OBIE Awards (one for playwriting for *Prelude to a Kiss* and another for his direction of Harry Kondoleon's *Saved or Destroyed*); the Outer Critic's Circle Award (*Prelude to a Kiss*); the Sundance Audience Award (*Longtime Companion*); a LAMBDA Award (for his TCG anthology *What I Meant Was*); and three Drama Desk nominations (*Reckless, Prelude to a Kiss* and *Missing Persons*). He also received a Tony nomination and was a Pulitzer finalist for *Prelude to a Kiss.* He is the recipient of two Rockefeller Foundation grants as well as a Guggenheim fellowship and an NEA/TCG Fellowship.

He recently directed Harry Kondoleon's *Play Yourself,* starring Marian Seldes, Elizabeth Marvel, Ann Guilbert and Juan Hernandez at New York Theatre Workshop. He is the Associate Artistic Director of the Intiman Theatre in Seattle, and is a contributing editor to *BOMB* magazine.

A graduate of Boston University, where he studied with poet Anne Sexton and historian Howard Zinn, Mr. Lucas lives in upstate New York with set designer John McDermott.